Jumpstarting Your Career

An Internship Guide for Criminal Justice

DOROTHY TAYLOR

University of Miami

Prentice Hall, Inc.
Upper Saddle River, NJ 07458

Library of Congress Cataloging-in-Publication Data

Taylor, Dorothy L., 1938-
   Jumpstarting your career : an internship guide for criminal
justice / Dorothy L. Taylor.
       p.   cm.
   Includes bibliographical references and index.
   ISBN 0-13-795857-9
   1. Criminal justice, Administration of--Study and teaching
(Internship)--United States.   I. Title.
HV9950.T38 1998
364.973'071'1--dc21

98-25933
CIP

Editorial/Production Supervision,
   Interior Design, and Electronic Paging: *Naomi Sysak*
Acquisitions Editor: *Neil Marquardt*
Cover Design: *Miguel Ortiz*
Manufacturing Buyer: *Ed O'Dougherty*
Managing Editor: *Mary Carnis*
Marketing Manager: *Frank Mortimer, Jr.*
Director of Production: *Bruce Johnson*

©1999 by Prentice-Hall, Inc.
Simon & Schuster/A Viacom Company
Upper Saddle River, New Jersey 07458

Printed in the United States of America

10 9 8 7 6 5 4 3 2 1

ISBN 0-13-795857-9

Prentice-Hall International (UK) Limited, *London*
Prentice-Hall of Australia Pty. Limited, *Sydney*
Prentice-Hall Canada Inc., *Toronto*
Prentice-Hall Hispanoamericana, S.A., *Mexico*
Prentice-Hall of India Private Limited, *New Delhi*
Prentice-Hall of Japan, Inc., *Tokyo*
Simon & Schuster Asia Pte. Ltd., *Singapore*
Editora Prentice-Hall do Brasil, Ltda., *Rio de Janeiro*

This book is dedicated
to the memories
of my daughter,
Sharon Doreen Hayes Lewis,
and my brother,
Fred Pitts, Jr.

Contents

Foreword

Internships in criminal justice serve many purposes. They provide students with insight into the day-to-day operations of a criminal justice professional agency and help students understand how knowledge gained in the classroom applies to the "real world" of the criminal justice system. It also allows them to assess their skills and abilities against the tasks of real-work situations. Internships can also provide students with connections for future employment and assist them in deciding on a particular area of interest. [See *Criminal Justice Internships* (http://www.runet.edu/-crju.web/internship.htm). Radford, VA: Radford University, Department of Criminal Justice, 1996.] However, internships are often hit-or-miss affairs, poorly planned and with little supervision and no follow-up. Students often do not know what to expect or how to proceed once they are assigned to agencies, and agencies frequently do not know what to do with the students. Many student interns report that they fetched coffee, did filing, and "observed" for their entire experience. Few would argue that such a situation is a meaningful educational experience. This book is designed to assist students in obtaining effective internships and successful transitions to employment in the professional world. It will also help internship supervisors and coordinators develop and administer challenging and productive educational experiences for students who are enrolled in criminal justice internships.

In this book, Dorothy Taylor, associate professor of criminology and sociology at the University of Miami, offers a plan for successful internship experiences. The author, who combines many years of experience in criminal justice and social service agencies with her tenure as the internship coordinator for the Criminology Program at the University of Miami, has written an exceptionally well-conceived "how to do it" manual for effective criminal justice internships. Her approach is multifaceted, stressing not only the student's role in the internship experience, but also the role and responsibilities of the criminal justice agencies involved, and of the university and faculty coordinator.

In Part I, Taylor presents an overview of the concept of internships from historical, philosophical, and theoretical perspectives. This broad view is followed by a discussion of how to develop goals and objectives for internships and how to assess progress toward these goals and objectives. The field-placement process is then examined, and suggestions are offered for selecting internship sites, ensuring the proper placement of students, and conducting placement interviews.

In Part II the agencies that offer internship placements, including their structure, bureaucratic concerns, and agency politics are examined. These insights into the internal operations of criminal justice agencies give both the student and the faculty coordinator information that should make the internship experience more meaningful.

Part III looks at the role of the student, the agency, and the faculty supervisor. Each of these topics is considered in detail, and important concerns for the internship experience are examined. One topic often missing from an internship syllabus is ethics. This section includes a chapter on the intern's value system and ethical principles for criminology and criminal justice.

Part IV offers a perspective on the student's, agency supervisor's, and the faculty coordinator's evaluations of the internship. The final chapter looks at careers in criminal justice, including instructions for preparing a résumé and investigating employment opportunities and suggestions for continuing education.

One unique feature of this book is the Resource Guide which catalogs criminal justice agencies in 25 major cities in the United States. This should prove to be a major benefit to students as they search for employment opportunities and for internship coordinators as they explore internship opportunities and placements.

In summary, this is an excellent and long-awaited manual for improving the internship experience in criminal justice education. I believe that it is a necessary educational tool for students and for the bookshelves of criminal justice educators.

Paul Cromwell, Ph.D.
Hugo Wall School of Urban and Public Affairs
University of Wichita
Wichita, Kansas
December 1997

Preface

This book was written for students in the social sciences (criminal justice, criminology, psychology, sociology, and social work) who are beginning a criminal justice internship in a public or private agency. It will also be a useful reference for faculty and agency supervisors. The book focuses on many issues involved in the total internship experience, especially those related to students' personal and professional development during their internship education. A guide of this sort is important because many of my students have, over the past six years, considered their internship among the most influential experiences of their undergraduate careers. At the same time, they have reported that their regular course work provides only indirect, and generally insufficient, preparation for their initial real-world experiences. This book is designed to make the connection between academic course work and the knowledge, skills, and emotional challenges that are found in the professional world of work.

Finding limited up-to-date information and materials on criminal justice internships, I decided to write this book after six years of testing the contents with criminology and sociology students interning in criminal justice and social service agencies. Because a world catalog search revealed that there was only one contending criminal justice internship book available and that the only other two publications were outdated (1967 and 1970), I also attempted to use the best information available from psychology, social work, and other disciplines that the interns will encounter in their various placements. I conducted extensive literature reviews of the leading journals and textbooks in each discipline and consulted with several faculty and agency supervisors in various colleges and universities and internship placements.

Using my personal experience as an intern and my experience coordinating internship placements for hundreds of students, I designed this book to be used as an introductory text on internships that can also be a helpful resource tool for students in their work at the agencies. I hope this book will help readers have a more effective and rewarding work and learning experience.

Acknowledgments

A number of people have influenced and contributed to the preparation of this book. For their encouragement and assistance, I would like to express my gratitude and appreciation to Professors Coramae Richey Mann and Paul Cromwell.

For substantive contributions in helping to shape this book, I would like to thank the many students who have taken my internship course, especially Alia Alinor, Simone Chai, Katherine Florian, Maritza Gutierrez, Mark Henderson, James Hinton, Mandi Homa, Christine Jean, Jodi Karsch, Jason Khoury, Dalyn Marrero, Duree Mellion, Joanna Pater, Andre Remy, and Gabriel Santos. In addition, I would like to thank Dalyn Marrero, Andre Remy, Katherine Florian, Alia Alinur, Christine Jean, Joanne Pater, Mandi Homa, Will Cobb, Tracy Julien, Jason Meringolo, Jill Osenkarski, Lisa Lee, and Claudine Francis for contributing chapter opener photos. Thanks also to Edmund and Susan Benson of the ARISE Foundation. I am especially grateful for the support from Robert Huling of Miami Federal Correctional Institute for providing numerous documents on prisons and camps and for suggestions on content that significantly enhanced Chapter 4.

Special thanks is extended to Wendy Almeleh for her editorial contributions, Perri Weinberg-Schenker for her assistance, Will Cobb and Tomeka Law for their computer skills, and Claudine Francis and Ana Villaraos for their contribution to the resource guide.

Finally, for their patience and understanding while I spent so many hours on the computer, at the library, and performing various other tasks involved in writing a book, a huge thanks to my husband, family, and friends.

The Concept of Internships

Long before there was big business, large government, or free-market enterprise, there were interns. In medieval times they were apprenticed to knights and blacksmiths. During the industrial age, children learned trades and skills at low or no pay from the master craftsmen. Thus, as long as there have been skills to learn, there have been interns of some sort.

Today, it is much the same. Stockbrokers, police officers, members of Congress, television producers, and educators are just a few of the persons who take interns under their wings and pass on practical knowledge of their businesses or professions. In addition, many states are in the process of enacting laws that will require prospective teachers to intern with mentors before they are considered for teaching certificates (Barnett, 1990).

An internship is as vital to current college students as is the regular curriculum. After she interviewed graduates, students, corporate recruiters, and placement directors, Scott (1992, p. 59) concluded that internships are "the single most effective college recruiting strategy."

Internships give students a much-needed foot in the door to their careers (Scott, 1992, p. 59). Internships also afford companies the opportunity to give prospective employees a semester- or summer-long tryout before deciding whether to hire them.

Indeed, internships are mutually beneficial to both students and organizations. However, not all internship placements are equally beneficial. How does an internship program ensure that students find the best placements for their future career goals? How does a student avoid being little more than a low- or no-paid gofer? These are essential questions in any overview of internships.

Field education courses at various colleges and universities are referred to by different titles, such as internships, practice, and fieldwork. Throughout this book, however, the terms *internship* and *field education* are used interchangeably.

Part I is devoted to exploring the concept of internships. Chapter 1 discusses why students should consider internships, the history of internships, the method of transferring theory into practice with self-directional learning, personal development in relation to coping skills, and professional development that is pertinent to values and ethics. Three common classifications characterize the field education process:

1. *Overview*, in which the student spends time in all branches of an agency to get an overall picture of the agency's function.
2. *Service delivery*, in which the student, under close supervision, actually deals with the agency's clients.
3. *Research*, in which the student uses the facilities of the agency as a laboratory for inquiry into a topic that the student and faculty supervisor have agreed upon. (Blackwelder and Moorman, 1975–1976, p. 2)

Chapter 2 focuses on realistic goal setting prior to starting a field placement, developing pragmatic educational objectives, and methods for assessing one's progress. Chapter 3 provides information on selecting and matching students with the best internship sites, preparing students for the background screening conducted by most criminal justice agencies, and the liability and insurance issues that arise in some agencies.

Defining Internships

Questions for Students

Why consider an internship?

What is the benefit of integrating classroom knowledge with practical experience?

What are the scholastic, personal, and professional advantages of an internship?

FIELD EDUCATION CONSIDERATION

Why should students consider internships? Although students may be confident that they want careers in criminology or criminal justice, they may not be sure of the specific area in which they wish to specialize. Internships will help them determine the most desirable areas for their future careers or indeed, decide whether they want to remain in the discipline at all. In addition, learning the management procedures of organizations affords significant insights into and understanding of the administration of various agencies. Furthermore, student interactions with agency supervisors, clients, and the agency staff constitute a comprehensive instructional experience that will prove invaluable and will aid in cultivating alliances that may be beneficial in obtaining employment in the future. In some instances, students may be employed by the agencies after the internships end.

HISTORY OF FIELD PLACEMENTS

Evidence of internships goes back to the Middle Ages, when apprenticeships were served with master craftsmen. This concept continues with field education in various scholastic areas, such as education, law, medicine, nursing, and social services. Several states require persons to undergo internships before they grant certification to practice in these respective disciplines.

From 1968 to 1980, when federal funds were available for internships in criminology and criminal justice, internships became a central component of higher instruction in the field. This funding enabled the Law Enforcement Assistant Administration (LEAA) to grant compensated internships for eight weeks or more at a salary of $65 per week for full-time students. This policy and the LEAA were discontinued in 1980 (Gordon and McBride, 1990).

Although paid criminal justice internships were no longer available, there were still unpaid internships in the field, and the popularity of internships, in general, grew by leaps and bounds during the "intern-crazy nineteen-eighties" (Scott, 1992, p. 59). During that decade competition increased. The baby boom was peaking, with students graduating from universities in droves and seeking employment. Major companies were eager to assist. Businesses such as Digital and Wang, which invested in in-house television studios and additional perks, also invested extravagantly in internship programs.

The abundance of college students and the extensive growth in business enabled corporations to offers internships, which gave them the opportunity to train, observe, and evaluate students for future employment. Summer internships became attractive ways for students to build their résumés.

In the early 1990s, after a decade of growth, the economy stagnated and business decreased, as did many internship programs. For some corporations, internship programs are no longer cost-effective. However, internships are still the most effective model for recruiting college graduates for entry-level positions. Therefore, businesses that decrease or abolish their internship programs are "short-sighted and stand to lose their competitive advantage on campus" (Scott, 1992, p. 60).

In addition, as Brenda Brassard, human resources manager for Fidelity Investments in Boston, noted: "Companies are doing less hiring, so the competition is fiercer for internships" (quoted in Wennes, 1993, p. 31). Internships have become significantly more difficult to obtain because there are more students than available positions. When they need to hire more personnel, businesses are more likely to hire those with the pragmatic experience that internships afford. Students are aware of this attitude. As a Wichita State engineering major, Gary Spexarth, said of his internship experience: "I learned a lot more than I ever will, or have, by going to school…it looks so much better when you graduate" (quoted in Wennes, 1993, p. 32).

FROM THEORY TO PRACTICE

Field education has become a central component of the instructional process, affording students a chance for hands-on experience with criminology and criminal justice practitioners. Furthermore, in internship courses, the didactic instruction received in the classroom is enriched, enhanced, and better understood through practical experience in the application of concepts, theories, and principles. (For the principles of internships, see Box 1.1.)

Much of a student's educational instruction occurs in the classroom and consists of note taking and discussion. Learning is restricted to the course content, the instructor's knowledge, the syllabus, and other students' contributions. In this setting, one may or may not choose to participate.

During an internship, the education process is guided by the student (Gordon and McBride, 1990:05). The instructional procedure is guided by actual situations (Dudley, 1980). In addition, examinations and rebuttal are eliminated from the evaluation process.

Although students can apply their knowledge directly and observe particular theories in practice, there may be some they may never observe. It is rewarding to hear from students: "I think internships should be required. The textbooks just don't tell the whole story. Those theories just don't prove out in the real world." For most students, the internships are the first time they are given the chance to test various theories of criminology in a professional setting. In addition, most internship courses require a term paper and several agencies request written narratives. Students' verbal and written communication skills usually improve, as do their listening and interviewing skills.

PERSONAL AND PROFESSIONAL DEVELOPMENT

During the course of their internships, students may be compelled to define, evaluate, or reevaluate their values. By becoming self-aware and learning about their own perspectives and capabilities, they will be able to cultivate the reliance and self-confidence that are crucial to problem solving. This process will be facilitated by their exposure to people who think, believe, and behave differently. These encounters, which are prevalent in many criminal justice agencies, may cause students to examine their own biases and opinions about social issues and become defensive because of their need to reject clients' different values and actions taken by criminal justice agencies. In any event, this exposure will stimulate passions and feelings associated with genuine life circumstances that cannot be generated in the classroom. Some understanding of causal elements in relation to people with problems should empower students to strengthen their convictions about the dignity and value of the persons they are learning to deal with. Assistance from faculty supervisors and agency supervisors should enable them to become more self-aware and thereby to move from subjectivity to objectivity when working with clients.

As interns, students will need to dress properly, maintain an acceptable image, and be dependable. The interns should be prompt, dependable, and efficient. They should also be aware of the significance of performing within an agency context and the necessity of communicating to people in all positions.

In addition to acquiring experience, internships enable students to determine if they really want to work in the field. Most students who approach me for internships

Box 1.1   PRINCIPLES OF INTERNSHIPS

Hal Blackwelder and Elliott Moorman, *Internships in Criminal Justice: A Guide to Service-Learning Internships in Agencies of North Carolina's Criminal Justice System.* Raleigh, NC: North Carolina Department of Administration, 1975–1976.

This booklet is an outgrowth of the Criminal Justice Recruitment and Service-Learning Project, sponsored by the North Carolina Department of Administration during the 1975–1976 academic year. The project was funded by the Governor's Commission on Law and Order with federal funds from LEAA. It was charged with creating new internships (using the model developed by the North Carolina Internship Office) in state and local criminal justice agencies and with cataloging and coordinating existing internship programs in the criminal justice system.

According to Blackwelder and Moorman, internships are a priceless tool in criminology and criminal justice training in that they give students the opportunity to combine information that they learn in the classroom with practical applications. A well-designed internship is an arrangement between a student, a faculty coordinator, and an agency supervisor. The authors stated that internships are based on seven principles (p. 23):

1. Each service-learning intern [should] have at least one *well-defined activity* that is regarded as worthwhile by the organization or group with whom the intern is affiliated, by the intern, and by the faculty mentor.

2. Each service-learning intern [should] develop *specific learning objectives* that can readily be identified and reviewed periodically throughout the work period. The support committee members of faculty and host organization representatives should also develop specific objectives for their participation.

3. Each intern or group of interns [should] be supported by a college-related faculty person and/or community or public organization person. The roles of these *support people* are to assist with task definition, learning objective definition, carrying out of the task, counseling with the intern, and carrying through with the ideas and projects initiated.

4. Each intern [should] *contract* as an independent agent with the organization involved to do the work and pursue the learning objectives in cooperation with a postsecondary educational institution.

5. Each intern [should] have adequate time for private reflection for *assessment* of the worth of his own experience in providing service to others and learning in a nonschool setting.

6. Each intern [should] produce a report or communication vehicle that is primarily for the agency with which he is affiliated.

7. Such a *product* should also be illustrative of the learning realized through the experience.

> Where possible, regular workshops or meetings [should] be required and arranged to make possible *student-to-student* feedback and accountability. [A learning team of ten to fifteen students meeting regularly (weekly) with supportive mentors is a proven and workable model for encouraging peer-group learning and support.]

are usually considering law school or work in criminal justice agencies (local and federal) or police departments or with delinquent youths. For the seven years that I have been an internship coordinator, most students complete their training with increased enthusiasm for their career goals. However, a few have found their selected areas unsuitable. For example, a student who was interested in working with delinquent youths reevaluated her goals after she completed her internship at an "alternative school" for juvenile delinquents. As she put it: "These kids are scary. I was afraid every day I was there. The only reason I stayed was because I was always with my supervisor [but] still got kicked one day. These kids are on drugs, they're sexually active, and have no respect for anyone. I've never been around adolescents like these. I had no idea how severe the problem is. I could never do this as a career."

Some of my students' internships have resulted in offers of employment with the organizations. However, such job offers are usually not the case. Nevertheless, the experience gained and knowledge about how to obtain jobs are invaluable, as are the references and contacts that students acquire.

In most cases, internship experiences are positive. However, in a few situations, the experiences are unsuccessful and the agencies refuse to provide references for preemployment background investigations, because of the intern's unethical conduct or personal and/or professional difficulties during fieldwork.

SUMMARY

Internship programs are the most effective model for recruiting college students for entry-level positions. Although financial subsidies are not automatic, college credits are earned, experience is gained, and invaluable contacts are made for future employment.

The objectives of internships are to help students:

1. Achieve firsthand knowledge and a better perception of criminal justice agencies, their management operations, and the neighborhood forces that influence their structure and procedures.
2. Acquire an awareness of the consequences of social abnormalities upon the public.
3. Combine and implement theories and other information gained in related courses with the practical experience afforded by the field placement.

4. Learn methods and skills that are used in criminal justice agencies, such as observation; organization; and effective communication, listening, and interviewing skills.

5. Develop self-awareness of their values and attitudes toward citizens, the criminal justice system, and the community at large.

Generally, internship programs are designed to assist the students to change their attitudes "from the subjective to the objective through the integration of theoretical class-room material with practical learning experiences" (Keyman, 1997, p. 10).

Because of variations in both students and agencies, not all interns will accomplish all these objectives. However, students may use these criteria to evaluate their pursuit of careers in criminology or criminal justice.

c h a p t e r   2

Goals and Instructional Objectives

Questions for Students

What field are your career goals related to?

Will the work experience in the agency help you achieve these goals?

After the internship, will you have sufficient credentials to qualify for an agency position?

TYPES OF GOALS

The accumulation of information, appraisal of accomplishments, individual develop-ment, and professional growth are four distinctive domains in which students should consider goals and instructional objectives.

The goal of *accumulating information* assists students in acquiring knowledge in areas they knew little about before their internships. It can be achieved, with the aid of the faculty supervisor and agency supervisor, by reading various publications and obtaining organizational information related to the field placement (see Box 2.1).

The goal of *appraising accomplishments* helps students estimate how adequately they have comprehended and performed the assignments of the field placement and the expertise they have acquired in certain skills. It is also necessary for the students to evaluate the conditions in their agencies, distinguish motives for alliances, and examine patterns. For instance, an intern working in the Florida Department of Corrections and Probation and assigned to "the above-standards hallway" (where officers are well

---

Box 2.1   One Student's Goals for Accumulating Information

Carol Lynn Cecil, "Summer Internship: Florida Department of Corrections and Probation," unpublished manuscript, 1996.

This unpublished paper is the result of an internship with the Florida Department of Corrections and Probation in Miami.

According to this, her goals for the accumulation of information were as follows (pp. 2, 8):

1. I would like to understand more about laws related to sex-offender incidents and the personalities of the judges hearing these cases.

2. I want to achieve a better comprehension of the different laws under which hundreds of independent agencies of the United States administer probation.

3. I want to understand why these agencies operate under different laws in every state and under various guidelines even within the same state.

---

organized and perform their jobs well) might establish a goal of developing rapport with these officers to learn more about the job cliques, the division of labor among various officers, and the methods they use to manage their clients better than do the officers in the "regular hallways" (Cecil, 1996).

The goal of *individual development* is attained from the opportunity to mature and develop during the internship process. In this regard, it is important for students to catalog their individual assets to discover their strengths and weaknesses. Assistance from "significant others" may help them clarify their individual-development goals.

The following are illustrations of individual development goals: (1) to learn to work with people from diverse backgrounds, (2) to become aware of how your values and ethics have been shaped by your background and how other people are influenced by theirs, (3) to improve your writing and language skills to increase self-confidence when interacting with supervisors, and (4) to become more assertive in relationship building with co-workers and peers.

The goal of *professional growth* is accomplished by selecting an internship placement relative to a possible career. These aspirations may be distinctive or vague. For example, a student may want a career as a secret service agent or with an organization that provides direct assistance to consumers. Many students whom I have advised have set the goal of acquiring experience as a law clerk in the office of the state attorney to confirm whether they want to attend law school and, if so, what area they wish to specialize in.

PRAGMATIC GOAL SETTING

Beginning interns should have gained basic information about criminology and other associated fields in the classroom and thus should have a solid theoretical foundation for understanding individuals, criminology, criminal justice, and society. It is likely that the student chose internships in criminology or criminal justice because they are considering careers in some facet of the discipline, such as law enforcement, corrections, or juvenile justice. During and after their internships, the students will probably ponder many questions related to their career goals, such as these: Was the work satisfactory? Were the agency environment and employee relationships enjoyable? Do I have adequate credentials to qualify for an open position at the agency? If so, do I consider the position a stepping-stone to other positions or a final position?

The students' choice of field placements will depend on their educational, practical, and specific goals. The apparent educational goals are:

- To grasp the procedures of the criminal justice profession
- To apply theories presented in the classroom to actual practice in the field
- To achieve training and gain contacts that will assist in successful transitions to employment in the professional world

The need to distinguish specific goals and to develop a technique for accomplishing them are essential if students are to realize what they have achieved during the field experience. For students to set practical and specific goals, they must first address personal-assessment questions, their skills, and geographic considerations. Furthermore, since most internships do not provide stipends, students need to consider whether they have sufficient funds from college loans and other sources to support themselves and, if applicable, their families during the internship period. Other issues are whether they prefer casework or group work and need constant stimulation or a more stable environment in which things remain pretty much the same from day to day. In establishing realistic goals, you should consider the following:

- The number of hours required at the internship agency
- The responsibilities that the agency will assign to you
- Your personal strengths and weaknesses
- Your skills and competence levels
- Your comprehension of the operations of the criminal justice system and your ability to transfer theory into practice

Once students determine the answers to these and other questions, they and the faculty supervisor can begin to match their criteria to those of various agencies and areas in which they are interested.

DEVELOPING EDUCATIONAL OBJECTIVES

After the students have established their goals in the four domains, they determine distinctive educational objectives to specify how they aim to achieve their goals. It is imperative that they confer with the agency supervisor and the faculty coordinator to guarantee that the objectives are practical, obtainable, and appraisable. The objectives serve as a guide to ascertaining the students' accountability at the placement site, as well as tools to measure the students' general achievement and as a foundation for dialogue during routine supervisory conferences.

The following are examples of educational objectives that may be established:

1. I will keep a weekly journal of my thoughts, feelings, and experiences from my internship.
2. I will discuss these issues with my agency (field) supervisor, my faculty supervisor, and the people I am assigned to work with.
3. I will get feedback from my agency supervisor regarding the impression the staff have of me to compare with how I think I am perceived by the staff.

An intern working in a probation department established the following educational objectives to achieve her goal of professional development:

1. I will learn about violation reports and drug tests from the officer assigned to these functions.
2. I will compare reports and confer with the officer regarding improvement.
3. I will continue to learn about violation reports and drug testing for the duration of my field experience.

Permaul (1981) noted that educational objectives for the goal of accumulating information should consist of the following:

1. Become aware of and informed about the topic.
2. Analyze, synthesize, and generalize the readings and discussions.
3. Take action or think about how you might act in specific situations.

An intern working in a center for girls in Dade County, Florida, wanted to understand more about sexual abuse, which many of the girls had encountered. She set the following objectives for achieving the goal of accumulating information:

1. I will review the sociological and criminological literature regarding the topic.
2. I will plan sessions with the staff social worker to gain a better understanding of the girls and sexual abuse.
3. I will confer with my agency supervisor to gain approval for conducting in-depth interviews with the sexually abused girls.

PROGRESS ASSESSMENT

Since the internship processes allows the students to become self-conducted learners, assessments of their progress in achieving their educational objectives and goals are their primary obligation. These tasks will assist the students to realize whether their goals and objectives are practical and obtainable in their field-placement settings.

Our students have found written assessments, audio- or videotaping, and feed-back to be helpful techniques:

1. *Written assessments* to your faculty supervisor in the form of notes, a journal, or e-mail will compel you to consider your experiences carefully and will provide you with a historical perspective as you progress through your internship.

2. *Audio- or videotaping* is also useful in evaluating your skills. Recording interviews with clients, victims, witnesses, and others can help you assess your competency, especially with assistance and feedback from your agency supervisor. You should explain to the person you are interviewing that you are recording the sessions, and obtain their written consent.

3. *Feedback* from supervisors and peers is another effective technique for evaluating your skills and competency levels. Feedback received from discussing your progress in regular meetings with your faculty and agency supervisors and in seminars with your peers may cause you to reevaluate your goals and develop new goals and objectives. On the basis of the feedback they may want to change their learning objectives and add new goals.

SUMMARY

Education is a continuous process, which should be perceived as transpiring through formal and informal procedures. The internship program illustrates the many techniques by which students can take part in the educational process. This chapter has focused on four major goals that several internship programs have considered necessary for forming field education experiences: accumulating information, appraising accomplishments, individual development, and personal growth. Once their goals are clarified, students must determine precise educational objectives that allow them to attain their goals and evaluate their progress.

Flexibility is key to a successful internship experience. A student should be ready to adjust his or her goals, if necessary, as the field-placement environment becomes familiar. The issues addressed in this chapter are important for students' personal and professional development during their internships. They will also be helpful in furthering professional development in future jobs, whether in criminal justice or social service agencies.

c h a p t e r   3

Field-Placement Process

Questions for Students

What are your long-term professional aspirations?

What courses have you taken that may be relevant to an internship?

Is your daily schedule conducive to the hours required by an internship?

SELECTING THE INTERNSHIP SITE

The first step in selecting the internship site is to consider which agency will provide the best experience relevant to your career goals. If you want to work in law enforcement, you should consider a placement in a local, state, or federal law enforcement agency. If juvenile delinquency is of interest to you, the juvenile justice system affords a myriad of placements, such as the juvenile court, alternative schools, and residential treatment facilities. Many internship programs provide placements within local areas near colleges or universities. However, in some instances, schools place students in out-of-state agencies.

If your college program provides statewide, regional, or out-of-state internships, you should consider and discuss these possibilities with your internship coordinator a semester or two before you intend to begin the internship. You will need to know about the placement procedure, academic prerequisites, and application deadlines. (For sample information on academic prerequisities, see Box 3.1.) You should keep in mind that most internships are not paid, although some agencies provide a small stipend if permitted by the school.

Box 3.1   REQUIREMENTS

In order to intern:

1. You must have completed Soc 101 and Soc 271.
2. You must have an overall GPA of 2.5 or higher.
3. You must decide what area of the field or which specific agency you would like to intern with.
4. You must turn in all required forms to the Internship Coordinator by the deadline specified.
5. You must register for Soc 365 (Internships) and pay for 6 semester hours of credit by the university's deadline date for fee payment.
6. You are required to complete 240 hours at your internship placement.
7. You are further required to complete a satisfactory term paper, on your agency, which will be due during final exam week.

For additional information, please contact the Internship Coordinator at (305) 284-6038.

In some schools the placements are the sole responsibility of the students, while in other schools individual departments control all components of the internship process. As I have done in the Sociology Department of the University of Miami, many internship coordinators have identified internship supervisors and sites that are used annually and require students to consider these placements first. However, if students find contacts for placements that are either more relevant to their career goals or closer to their homes, the coordinator may consider these placements after they visit and approve the sites and appoint staff supervisors. The final decision for the internship placement should be *yours*.

PROPER STUDENT PLACEMENT

Once the site has been selected, the process of matching you with a site plays an important role in guaranteeing a positive experience for both you and an agency. I schedule half-hour appointments for each perspective intern to discuss matching. Some students are not sure of their career goals at the time, and after some discussion, I advise them to schedule another appointment when they have thought through the options more clearly. You should approach this process attentively, so that your initial internship experience is positive. Since you will be spending a good deal of your time (from two to four days a week) and resources on this endeavor, you have the right to get the most benefit from it.

Over the years, I obtained information pertinent to efficient and successful matching from students during our interviews. On the basis of Baird's (1996) model, I then generated an information form for collecting data on students' characteristics for matching interns with placement sites. Matching these data with information from various agencies increases the probability that the placements will be successful.

THE FIELD-PLACEMENT INTERVIEW

You have been notified that your paperwork has been received and processed by the agency and that you have been accepted for an interview. The interview is the second important step in the placement process because it gives you the opportunity to have a one-to-one discussion with the agency supervisor and occasionally with other significant personnel who will be involved in the selection process. This is the time to address issues, concerns, and questions regarding the agency's responsibilities and yours as an intern. The interview is a crucial point because if the outcome is not satisfactory for either party, one or both can decide that the placement seems unsuitable. In some cases, either the student or the agency does not determine that the placement is unsuitable until a week or so into the internship. In such a case, some schools may be willing to reassign the student to another agency, only under extraordinary circumstances, but the agency has to be one that does not require an extensive background check and could accommodate the student in making up any lost hours to fulfill the internship credits.

To make a good impression at your interview, you should thoroughly research the organization's history, missions, and functions. You may obtain such information on the Internet, from the library, by visiting the agency, and by discussions with your internship coordinator and/or other students who have interned at the agency; in some colleges, coordinators may have brochures on several agencies. In addition, you should dress properly, by which I mean that a young man should wear a dress shirt, a tie, a suit or sports jacket, and dress shoes, and a young woman should wear a dress or suit (in warm climates, you may dispense with a jacket). When in doubt, check with your internship coordinator.

It should be noted that the proper dress for interviewing may not be the proper dress for work once you receive the internship. This is one of the issues that should be addressed during the interview. In some juvenile residential facilities, the preferred dress is jeans, T-shirts, and sneakers, while in other juvenile programs (such as Guardian Ad Litem in Miami), a dress or suit is required because of the short notice given for court appearances.

To avoid a negative image during the interview, *do not* chew gum, smoke, or wear strong perfume or after-five clothing. *Do not* be late; arrive at least 5 to 10 minutes early for your appointment. If you feel the need to take along a friend or someone has to drive you, leave the person in the reception area and go into the interview alone.

The potential supervisor will have a number of questions for you. You should also be prepared with questions regarding the internship. Some authors (Hersh and Poey, 1987; Pitts, 1992) have offered useful suggestions for prospective interns in preparing for interviews. For example, they have suggested that you:

- Describe to the interviewer why you want to work in this particular agency and what your goals there will be.
- Inquire about your expected duties, duties performed by former interns, and the hours and shift you would be assigned.
- Ask your interviewer about his or her experience as a professional and training and experience as a supervisor.

Some students have expressed anxiety regarding the interviewing process. Role-playing the interview with your coordinator or others or speaking with a student who previously interviewed at the agency will help to ease some of the anxiety.

Informal Background Check

In most internship programs, the internship coordinator conducts an initial screening to determine a student's eligibility for an internship. Then, depending on the type of agency and its policy, the agency providing the internship often does a second background check. All criminal justice agencies require background checks. The program's screening focuses on the student's academic standing, background information (previous course work) related to the placement, and individual responsibility, as well as evaluations by the faculty. The agency's screening is usually much more extensive. For example, one of my students who was applying for an internship with the U.S. Secret Service told me that his brother was in the armed forces and stationed in Germany (information that he included in his Secret Service application), so during the agency's background check the student's brother and wife were investigated.

After you have submitted your application, résumé, and cover letter, and have been interviewed, there is still a possibility that you may have to submit additional information about your background or give authorization for a background check. This is another reason why it is important to be truthful on the initial application that you submit to your internship coordinator. Affirmative action and antidiscrimination laws can prevent most agencies in the public and private sectors from asking questions that are not job related. Law enforcement and other criminal justice agencies, however, have more leeway in their background investigations, and some agencies use polygraph tests to check on personal practices and criminal history, honesty, and reliability. Drug and alcohol use may also be checked, and some agencies may ask you to submit to drug testing.

The background check is a serious matter. If you are truly interested in a career in the field of criminal justice or the discipline of criminology, you must constantly avoid unethical or criminal conduct.

THE AGENCY SCREENING PROCESS

Just as you are considering whether an agency is an appropriate placement for you, an agency's administrators also have to decide if you are eligible to be an intern for the agency. In making this decision, the administrators will review your application, cover letter, résumé and transcript; interview you; and check your background. Therefore, you should be prepared for all these aspects of the selection process.

Completing an Application, Résumé, and Cover Letter

If the application is a standard form, you should type or print it and complete it as thoroughly as possible. You should then submit it to your internship coordinator six to eight weeks prior to the beginning of the proposed internship or in whatever time frame the coordinator deems necessary. (For a sample application, see Figure 3.1.)

The school's application usually asks for the following information: the semester and year of the requested internship, personal demographics, grade-point average, whether you have a driver's license and have an automobile at your disposal, whether

---

SEMESTER/YEAR YOU WOULD   DATE OF APPLICATION
LIKE TO INTERN_____   _____
NAME_____   SS# _____
LOCAL
ADDRESS_____   PHONE _____
PERMANENT
ADDRESS_____   PHONE _____

YEAR IN SCHOOL _____   DOB_____   OVERALL G.P.A _____
DO YOU HAVE A CAR? _____   GRADUATION DATE _____
HAVE YOU COMPLETED: YES   NO   TAKING NOW   GRADE
SOC 101 (INTRO TO SOCIOLOGY)   _____   _____ _____   _____
SOC 271 (INTRO TO CRIM JUSTICE)   _____   _____ _____   _____

WHERE DO YOU WISH TO INTERN? _____
NAME OF PERSON IN CHARGE OF INTERNS AT THE
AGENCY _____
ADDRESS OF AGENCY _____
_____PHONE _____
MANY AGENCIES MAY NOT ACCEPT STUDENTS WITH CONVICTIONS. IN ORDER
TO FACILITATE PLACEMENT, PLEASE ANSWER THE FOLLOWING:

HAVE YOU EVER BEEN CONVICTED OF A FELONY OR A FIRST-DEGREE MISDE-
MEANOR?
YES _____NO _____
IF YES, PLEASE SPEAK WITH THE COORDINATOR PRIOR TO PLACEMENT.

LIST MOVING VIOLATIONS (i.e., speeding, careless driving, etc.)
_____
_____

6 CREDIT HOURS (MINIMUM 240 HOURS AT AGENCY AND TERM PAPER).

YOU MUST SIGN THIS APPLICATION. A FALSE STATEMENT ON ANY PART OF THIS
APPLICATION MAY BE GROUNDS FOR NOT RECEIVING AN INTERNSHIP PLACE-
MENT, OR FOR BEING TERMINATED FROM AN AGENCY AFTER PLACEMENT. ALL OF
MY STATEMENTS ARE MADE IN GOOD FAITH, AND ARE TRUE AND COMPLETE.

_____   _____
STUDENT SIGNATURE   DATE

Figure 3.1   Sample Internship Application

you have taken courses that are prerequisites for an internship, desired agency, and record of violations. It is important that you sign the application in good faith because a false statement can be grounds for termination.

The résumé and cover letter should also be submitted to your internship coordinator within the specified period. This material, along with other pertinent information, will be forwarded to the agency that is considering your placement. After the agency has reviewed your file and considered you an acceptable candidate, you will probably have to complete another application for the agency. The internship coordinator may provide a standard résumé as a guide. (See Figure 3.2 for a sample résumé form.)

NAME_____ SS# _____
LOCAL ADDRESS_____
_____
TELEPHONE _____MARITAL STATUS_____
DATE OF BIRTH_____YEAR IN SCHOOL_____
EDUCATION
HIGH SCHOOL _____
DATE GRADUATED_____
COLLEGE _____
MAJOR _____MINOR _____GPA_____
SOCIOLOGY COURSES COMPLETED (COURSE NUMBER AND TITLE):
_____   _____
_____   _____
_____   _____
                                          _____
SCHOLASTIC AWARDS, STUDENT ORGANIZATIONS, HOBBIES, INTERESTS
_____
_____
WORK EXPERIENCE (EMPLOYER'S NAME, ADDRESS, AND TELEPHONE)
____/___TO___/___ _____
                  _____
                  POSITION_____
____/___TO___/___ _____
                  _____
                  POSITION_____
____/___TO___/___ _____
                  _____
                  POSITION_____
REFERENCES:
1. Name/Title_____PHONE #(_____) _____
    Address: _____
2. Name/Title_____PHONE #(_____) _____
    Address: _____
3. Name/Title_____PHONE #(_____) _____
    Address: _____

Figure 3.2   Sample Student Internship Résumé

On this form you provide personal data, educational data, information on awards and hobbies, employment history, and references. Even though this form of résumé is acceptable, I recommend that you compose and type an individual résumé. It makes a better impression and will give you experience that you will need later in competing in the job market. (See Figure 3.3 for a sample typed résumé.)

Mandi A. Homa

Current Address: **Permanent Address:**
1228 Dickinson Drive, Apt. 32F   5010 Cotton Valley
Coral Gables, FL 33146   St. Croix, U.S.V.I.00820
(305) 663-6908   (809) 773-9282
MHOMA@STUDENTS.MIAMI.EDU

OBJECTIVE   Desire an entry-level public service position that builds upon psychology and criminology skills

EDUCATION   **UNIVERSITY OF MIAMI** Coral Gables, FL
                     Bachelor of Arts, May 1997, Majors: Psychology/Criminology,
                     Minor: Business Administration
                     Major GPA: 3.32/3.54, Overall GPA: 3.30

RELEVANT   **CRIMINOLOGY**
COURSES   Criminology: Law and Society   Criminal Justice
                     Criminology: Corrections   Juvenile Delinquency
                     Theories of Deviant Behavior   Minorities: Crime and Social Policy

                     PSYCHOLOGY
                     Abnormal Psychology   Psychology of Women
                     Psychobiology   Emotion
                     Psychology of Drugs and Behavior   Industrial and Organizational Psychology

                     BUSINESS ADMINISTRATION
                     Financial Accounting   Managerial Accounting
                     Fundamentals of Finance   Marketing Foundations
                     Organizational Behavior

SKILLS   • Windows 3.1
                     • Microsoft Word 6.0/Word Perfect
                     • Data Entry/Word Processing
                     • Organizational Skills
                     • Teaching Skills
                     • Able to work with children

HONORS   • Phi Alpha Delta, Pre-Legal Society
AND ACTIVITIES   • Dean's List
                     • Gamma Phi Beta Sorority
                     • Hurricanes Help the Hometown: Helped with hurricane recovery
                     • Food for Thought: Collected food for homeless

---

Figure 3.3   Sample Résumé

Regardless of which type you select, the résumé should be typed, properly spaced, and contain no typographical errors. (This internship résumé should be modified when you apply for paid positions.) Ideally, the résumé should be one page and should not exceed two pages.

When you apply for an internship (or other position), the cover letter should indicate why you have chosen the agency; what special knowledge, skills, or training you will bring to the agency; and what you expect to learn at the agency. *Do not treat the cover letter lightly*; it is an important consideration for the agency in arriving at a placement decision. (See Figure 3.4 for a sample cover letter.)

WORK EXPERIENCE January 97–Present	**FEDERAL BUREAU OF PRISONS** Miami, FL Student Intern • Involved in the daily operation of a Federal Bureau of Prisons Community Corrections Office • Assist staff in evaluating referrals of inmates from federal institutions • Assist in assigning inmates to appropriate community corrections center • Assist in evaluating program-related activities such as permission to drive and home confinement • Assist in evaluating community corrections center's performance regarding contract compliance, including evaluation of prerelease programs personnel and facility
Sept. 93–Dec. 96	**UNIVERSITY OF MIAMI ATHLETIC BUSINESS OFFICE** Coral Gables, FL • Student Assistant • Data Entry • Directed phone calls and recorded messages • Filed budget reports and other financial documents • Designed and organized a variety of filing systems
May 96–Aug. 96	**PRICE CLUB** St. Croix, U.S.V.I. Cashier/Salesperson • Operated cash register and responsible for accounting money • Sold Men's, Women's, and Childen's clothing • Set up displays and priced merchandise
Fall 88–Winter 94	**EQUESTRIAN INSTRUCTOR** St. Croix, U.S.V.I. • Instructed children and adults on how to care for and ride horses • Prepared both horse and rider for competitions and accompanied them to the competitions
Apr. 92–Aug. 93	**ST. CROIX FOOD CLUB** St. Croix, U.S.V.I. Deli Manager • Responsible for opening and closing deli • Received new shipments and prepared them for sale • Trained other employees • Bagged, weighed, and labeled meats and vegetables
REFERENCES	Available upon request.

Figure 3.3   (Cont'd)

1228 Dickinson Drive, Apt. 32F
Coral Gables, FL 33146
December 13, 1996

Ms. Andrea Johnson
Community Corrections Manager
Federal Bureau of Prisons
401 North Miami Avenue
Miami, FL 33178

Dear Ms. Johnson:

I am writing to express my interest in the student intern position that is available. I am currently a senior at the University of Miami and will be receiving my degree in both Criminology and Psychology in May, 1997.

I am very interested in a career in criminal justice and would enjoy working for the federal government after graduation. This internship will give me an opportunity to learn more about the criminal justice system. I have been working in an office for over three years. I am responsible for data entry, filing, organizing, and other things that will be helpful to your office.

I am very excited about the prospect of interning with your office. I look forward to hearing from you. Thank you for your consideration.

Sincerely,

Mandi Homa

Mandi Homa

Figure 3.4   Sample Cover Letter

Your internship coordinator may send a standard cover letter with your documents. However, if the cover letter is your responsibility, remember that it is your introduction to the agency. Therefore, address the letter to a specific person (whose name you may obtain from the coordinator), be brief, and make sure that all words are spelled correctly.

If your coordinator is handling this internship, he or she will receive the response from the agency, and in some instances you will also. If you are handling the internship and have not received a reply within two to three weeks, it is appropriate to inquire, by telephone or mail, about the status of your application. This contact should be made with the person to whom you addressed the cover letter.

LIABILITY COVERAGE

Since internship courses have become a central part of several social science degree programs, they have heightened universities' and internship agencies' concern about liability issues (Schultz, 1992). Thus, there seems to be a need for mutual under-standing between universities and agencies of the legal responsibilities and potential liabilities of each. As Schultz (1992) pointed out, both parties to an internship agree-ment have the right to be informed of the legal implications; knowledge of potential liabilities can alert program directors to methods for minimizing unnecessary risks and managing them effectively. Also, information about liability issues can alleviate the concerns of placement supervisors at agencies, who may be cautious about under-taking such arrangements unless they understand these issues at the outset.

The main concern of the internship coordinator and the university is injury to the student while at the field placement or while involved in internship-related activities. The decision about whether you can participate in various placement activities is the sole responsibility of your field supervisor. You, however, have the right to decline to participate in any event that you think is unsafe. Before you begin an internship, the coordinator may discuss safety guidelines that are pertinent to your placement. For instance, all U.S. police departments and schools have agreements that students who participate in "ride-alongs" are not permitted outside the patrol cars or to be in areas where officers respond to violent encounters. In addition, students who intern for the bureau of prisons are not allowed to enter the cell blocks or recreational facilities unescorted, and those who intern at the juvenile court are not allowed to conduct home visits unaccompanied.

You will probably be required by your internship coordinator and your field placement supervisor to sign a consent form that you have been informed of the inherent dangers of the internship and are releasing the school and/or the agency from liability. (See Figure 3.5 for a sample student agreement, including a release-of-liability clause.) These forms serve to signify a mutual understanding of the risks involved in interning. Black (1987) and Schultz (1992), however, warned that these forms are not completely binding against future legal actions or recovery.

Schultz (1992) suggested that it is necessary for students to receive insurance protection, but that obtaining such insurance can be complicated because of unique problems associated with health care, workers' compensation, and personal liability. Here I should point out that during my seven years as an internship coordinator, no stu-dent, agency, or my school has been sued for an alleged act of misfeasance or malfeasance.

Since health care insurance is not provided for interns at most placement sites, you should make sure that your university's student health plan provides appropriate coverage. If you are a part-time student, you should discuss the issue with an appro-priate school advocate.

Regarding workers' compensation, as a general rule, if you are receiving a stipend for services rendered to the agency, you would be covered. However, because the laws vary from state to state, it would be wise to seek expert opinion within your local area.

SUMMARY

Before deciding on your internship placement, you should have some idea of your long-term goals, even if they change in the future. It is always helpful if you have taken courses relevant to your desired internship. Another consideration is whether your schedule will allow you time to participate in an internship.

This statement is to affirm my understanding of the conditions under which I am applying for a Criminal Justice Internship in the Department of Sociology at the University of Miami.

I understand that in order to intern I must:

1. Have a completed SOC 101 and SOC 271;
2. Have at least an overall G.P.A. of 2.5;
3. Complete 240 hours at the internship placement;
4. Agree to complete the term paper assigned by the Internship Coordinator and made a part of my permanent file.

I understand that during my internship I will not be identified as anything other than a student intern, and I agree not to place myself or allow myself to be placed in dangerous situations nor allow myself to be used in any undercover capacity. Further, I agree to release the University of Miami and the Department of Sociology and the officers and faculty of same from all legal liability for any injury that I may sustain during the performance of activities as a student intern.

I understand that in order to fulfill the academic requirements of the internship program, I must:

(1) Complete a participant-observation type term paper in a satisfactory evaluation(s) and timely manner;

(2) Receive satisfactory evaluation(s) from my intern supervisor.

I further understand that my failure to fulfill these requirements will result in an unsatisfactory grade for the internship course.

I hereby accept these conditions under which my application for a criminal justice internship is being made.

Signed:_____

Date:_____

Figure 3.5   Sample Student Agreement

Many students are not sure of their career goals when choosing their placements. If you are not certain of your goals, schedule an appointment with the internship coordinator in your department and receive guidance.

The locations of internships vary from school to school. Some coordinators provide placements within local areas while others provide regional and out-of-state internships.

Although many coordinators have a list of participating agencies, they also are open to students suggesting and arranging new internship placements and supervisory contacts.

Criminal justice agencies perform in-depth background investigations, including family members and friends.

The three most important forms required by internship coordinators are the résumé, the cover letter, and the background application. One of each is included in this chapter.

During the agency interview, you will make a good impression by having some basic knowledge of the organization and perhaps of the agency supervisor. It is appropriate for you to inquire about the amount of time the supervisor will have to work directly with you. The proper attire for this occasion is a tie and a jacket for young men and a dress or suit for young women. Depending on the agency, the proper interviewing attire may not be the proper work attire. This issue should be addressed during the interview.

The intensity of the background screening depends on the agency's policy. The Secret Service screens more thoroughly than the probation department because these agencies have different levels of responsibility. The background check is a serious matter. To secure a career in the criminal justice field, your behavior must be above reproach, and you must avoid unethical or criminal conduct.

With regard to liability and insurance, the main concern of the internship coordinator and school is injury to the student. Although your field supervisor decides whether you can participate in placement activities, it is your right to decline to engage in any activity that you deem unsafe.

You will be asked by your internship coordinator and agency supervisor to sign a "hold harmless" consent form that you have been informed of the inherent dangers of the internship and are releasing the school and/or agency for any liability.

Health care insurance is not provided for interns at most placement sites. Generally, worker's compensation is considered only if you are a full-time intern and are receiving a stipend and are injured on the job. Because laws regarding workers' compensation vary from state to state, you should seek expert opinion regarding this issue.

Field Placement

The client population served is frequently foremost on the minds of the interns when selecting placements. At that time, consideration should also be given to the various types of internship settings available. For example, although the ages of the clients may be the same, an internship in an alternative school setting (for juvenile delinquents only) differs a great deal from an internship in a residential adolescent treatment facility. Similarly, although several of clients served, and the procedural methods used in correctional unsteadiness may be similar to those of a county jail, there will be significant differences that are distinctive to each type of setting. Therefore, it might be advantageous to know which of these settings have a formal or informal structure, and which structure you would be most comfortable working in. Consider, however, that aside from the clients served and the procedural methods used, if you only have training in one type of setting, an experience in a completely different setting could also be very informative. If you already have experience in a setting with a formal structure, I would encourage you to consider seeking an internship placement in an informal setting and see what there is to learn from another perspective, recognizing how the organizational structure of the agency influences the intern's field experience.

As an intern, you will also see how the organization of the agency influences the behavior of the staff. Chapter 4 will examine some of the organizational factors that will influence your performances at the internship setting and your relationship with clients. Chapter 5 discusses general agency concerns such as politics and finance, and Chapter 6 provides pertinent information on agency relationships.

c h a p t e r   4

Structural Characteristics

Questions for Students

How does the organizational structure of your agency affect your internship experience?

What effect does the formal structure have on your performance with clients?

How do the formal and informal structures influence your relationships with your supervisor and staff?

TYPES OF STRUCTURE

During your internship you will discover whether the structural characteristics of the agency in which you are working are formal or informal. Formal organizational structures provide fixed rules, regulations, and codes of conduct that pertain to the management of agencies and employees' relationships, whereas informal organizational structures do not. Informal structures are discussed later in the chapter. The characteristics of formal organizational structures will be of greater significance to you because they are found in the majority of criminal justice agencies.

THE FORMAL AGENCY STRUCTURE

Nigro and Nigro (1977), expanding the work of Max Weber, a nineteenth-century sociologist who introduced the characteristics of formal organizational structures with an emphasis on the role of bureaucracy in industrialized societies, suggested that even with its negative connotations, such as politics and red tape, bureaucracy refers to a particular pattern of social organization for managerial purposes. Without a doubt, bureaucracy is the most prominent form of organization for the administration of criminal justice agencies. Over the years, interns in our program have found Weber's characteristics of a formal organizational structure—the *hierarchical model, division of labor, rules and regulations, career orientation, efficiency and effectiveness, impersonal orientation*, and *communication*—operating in several agencies.

The Federal Bureau of Prisons, the Office of the State Attorney, the Public Defender's Office, and the Secret Service are the best known criminal justice sites with formal structures. In this chapter we discuss these characteristics in relation to the organizational structure of the Federal Bureau of Prisons' Federal Correctional Institute (FCI) of Miami. FCI facilities throughout the United States have similar organizational structures, but the respective departments under an associate warden may vary.

The Federal Bureau of Prisons is a Federal Corrections Agency under the U.S. Department of Justice. The prison, the FCI of Miami, consists of two separate facilities: the medium- security prison (FCI), surrounded by a tall wire fence (see Figure 4.1 for its organizational structure), and the minimum-security camp [the Federal Prison Camp (FPC)] without fences (see Figure 4.2 for its organizational structure). Both facilities are under the control of the same warden. The FPC administrator reports directly to the warden and is not accountable to either of the two associate wardens (the associate warden of operations or the associate warden of programs) for supervision purposes. The FPC is better known as a "satellite" camp to the FCI; it is not an autonomous operation. Approximately 800 inmates are housed in the FCI, and approximately 328 are housed in the FPC (as of July 1997, there were 794 FCI inmates and 333 FPC inmates, totaling 1127).

In 1970, in response to the public's concerns about prisons and inmates, the Bureau of Prisons set forth four primary objectives:

1. To increase program alternatives for offenders who do not require traditional institutional confinement, thereby minimizing the corrosive effects of imprisonment, lessening their alienation from society and reducing the economic costs to the taxpayer.

2. To enhance the quality of correctional staff by increased training opportunities, better working conditions, and heightened professional challenges to inspire continuous personal growth and satisfaction.

3. To improve present physical plants and incorporate new facilities into the system to increase the effectiveness of correctional programs.

4. To expand community involvement in correctional programs and goals because, in the final analysis, only through successful reintegration into the community can the ex-offender avoid reverting to crime. (Carlson 1994, p. 17)

The development of minimum-security camps (FPCs) also began in 1970. The purpose of these facilities was to reduce overcrowding and provide a more humane environment with better living conditions and low security for inmates who do not

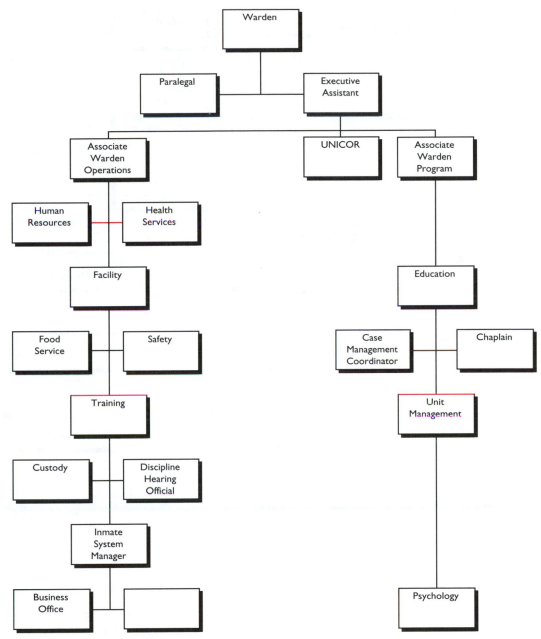

Figure 4.1   FCI Miami, Florida Organizational Chart: Formal Structure

require as much structure and supervision. The camps are small military-like barracks with open dormitories; they were constructed to provide only the physical security commensurate with inmates' needs, and at much lower expense, in the hope of reducing institutional violence, thereby enhancing the safety of staff members and inmates.

Figure 4.2   FCI Miami,
Florida Camp Organizational
Chart

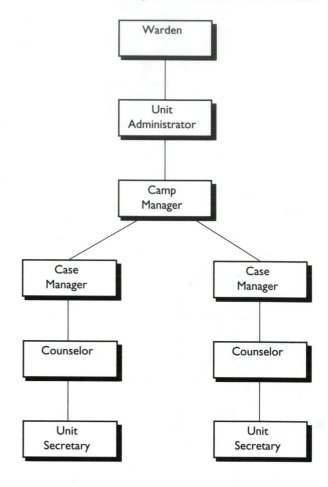

The original camps were established at the FCI in Lompoc, California, and the U.S. Penitentiary in Leavenworth, Kansas. There are presently 42 camps throughout the United States; see Box 4.1 for their locations. In the next section we compare the formal organizational structure of FCIs to Weber's (1947) characteristics.

Weber's Hierarchical Model

In this model, offices and positions are organized in a hierarchy with each office or position managed and supervised by a higher authority. The organizational chart formally operationalizes this characteristic and distinguishes and protects the levels of subordination among staff members, sections, offices, and departments.

FCI-Miami's Hierarchical Model   At the head of the organization is the warden, who serves as the chief executive officer of FCI and FPC. The warden plans, directs, and coordinates institutional programs in all functional areas within the framework of

Box 4.1	FORTY-EIGHT MINIMUM-SECURITY SATELLITE CAMPS TO THE FCI (AS OF JULY 1997)		
Location	Current Population	Rated Capacity	Percent Over or Under the Capacity
Ashland, GA	214	296	−28
Atlanta, GA	410	488	−16
Bastrop, TX	134	122	10
Beckley, WV	213	384	−45
Big Springs, TX	148	144	3
Butner, NC	285	296	−4
Carswell, TX	163	148	10
Cumberland, MD	261	256	2
Danbury, CT	202	178	13
Dubin, CA	243	299	−19
El Reno, OK	213	216	−1
Elkton,	147	256	−43
Englewood, CO	105	111	−5
Estill, SC	248	256	−3
Fairton, NJ	67	65	3
Florence, CO	379	512	−26
Greenville, IL	243	256	−5
Jessup, GA	411	508	−19
La Tuna, TX	229	246	−7
Leavenworth, KS	308	398	−23
Lewisburg, PA	244	352	−31
Lexington, KY	207	193	−7
Lompoc, CA	339	276	23
Loretto, PA	76	93	−18
Manchester, KY	364	512	−29
Marianna, FL	312	296	5
Marion, IL	291	310	−6
McKean, PA	260	292	−11
Memphis, TN	271	296	−8
Miami, FL	333	260	28
Oakdale, LA	140	118	19
Otisville, NY	91	100	−9
Oxford, WI	155	156	−1
Pekin, IL	294	256	15
Petersburg, VA	277	296	−6
Phoenix, AZ	221	272	−19
Schuylkill, PA	274	296	−7
Sheridan, OR	473	512	−8
Talladega, AL	368	296	24
Terre Haute, IN	336	340	−1
Texarkana, TX	349	220	59
Three Rivers, TX	285	256	11

Source: Miami FCI Procedure Manual.

the broad policies of the Federal Bureau of Prisons and directs the functional programs of the associate wardens and the camp administrator.

Directly below the warden are two associate wardens (one for operations and one for programs), the executive assistant, and the superintendent of industries (listed as UNICOR on the organizational chart). Both associate wardens plan, organize, supervise and evaluate programs in assigned areas of responsibility and serve as advisers and assistants to the warden in determining and establishing policies, programs, and procedures that affect all institutional operations. The executive assistant serves as the public information officer, preparing reports, coordinating tours for upper-division-level college students and persons employed in the federal law enforcement field, and developing and maintaining ongoing cooperative relations with community, civic, social, and welfare organizations. The superintendent of industries is responsible for the operation of the Textile Cut and Sew Factory (UNICOR), which manufactures cotton products. The functions of this position include ordering and storing, manufacturing and shipping all items that are produced. UNICOR is a private industry that operates in the prison to provide employment to inmates (sewing towels and linens, which are sold to the hospitality industry) who wish to work and send money home to their families.

The FPC administrator (who does not appear on the organizational chart) plans, organizes, supervises, and evaluates operations and programs at the FPC and serves as an adviser to the warden in determining and establishing policies, programs, and procedures at the camp.

Below the associate warden for operations is the facility administrator, followed by the training manager and the inmate systems manager. The training manager is responsible for employee development. The inmate systems manager oversees the processing of inmate commitments and release dates, the recording of legal and personal data, and the operation of the institutional mailroom.

Below the associate warden for programs is the educational-recreational administrator, followed by the unit managers and the director of psychology. The educational-recreational administrator is responsible for hiring and supervising teachers to teach elementary- and high-school-level courses to the inmates or to supervise the inmates' self-study programs and to provide an organized program of recreational, leisure-time activities for all inmates.

The multidisciplinary unit managers (who are equal in rank and authority) provide professional case management services to the inmates in their units and have administrative authority over all within-units aspects of inmates' lives. Each unit is semiautonomous, and each unit manager is responsible for counseling, supervision, institutional classification and programming, parole, helping inmates resolve their problems with institutional life, and developing release plans. The director of psychology is responsible for providing the full range of mental health services to the staff and inmates: applying psychological principles, techniques, theories, methods, and data to practical situations and problems; providing training and consultative services to the administrators; and assisting in the interdisciplinary classification of the inmates.

With the exception of UNICOR, this chart is a fair representation of most FCIs under the Bureau of Prisons. Other criminal justice agencies may have more or fewer levels of hierarchy, depending on their size.

Weber's Division of Labor

In a formal organizational structure, specific activities may be assigned to certain people according to their skills, discipline, education, and competence.

FCI-Miami's Division of Labor   Whereas the warden and the associate wardens have overall managerial duties in the prison, specific areas of the institution's management are assigned to administrators, managers, and other members of the professional and correctional staffs. Some of the areas delineated in the organizational chart (Figure 4.1) are facility management, training, inmate systems management, human resources, health services, food services, safety/occupational health, custody, the disciplinary hearing officer, and the business office. The heads of these departments are equal in rank and authority. Other criminal justice agencies may have fewer or more employees involved in the division of labor relative to their purpose in their organizations.

Weber's Rules and Regulations

The organization must have rules and regulations (usually referred to as office policies) that structure the daily operational guidelines (usually in the form of an operational or training manual) of the organization and establish the rights of and responsibilities for each job.

FCI-Miami's Rules and Regulations   All employees must go through an intensive three-week course about the bureau at Glynco, Georgia, that covers three main areas: academics, firearms training, and self-defense. A training manual, which includes program statements and local institutional supplements, is also given to all new employees. The program statement informs employees of the objectives, purpose, scope, and responsibilities of positions with the Federal Bureau of Prisons. The program statement regarding ethics and staff code of conduct is taken seriously; if an employee violates the code of conduct, he or she may be subject to disciplinary action ranging from a reprimand to removal. The training manual contains rules and regulations ranging from personal conduct, including a dress code, to information on filling out forms and using templates for letters and other documents.

Since FCI-Miami is a prison, its training manual also includes state penal laws, criminal procedure codes, and administrative regulations by state and federal agencies. Among others, an extremely important rule at FCI-Miami is *documentation*. As one of my interns reported: "I have to document everything! Something as minimal as pulling out a file to read. I have to fill out a form which asks for the name of the inmate, his register number, your name, the date and time you pulled the file, and your signature. Upon returning the file, the time returned and a signature is required."

If you are interning for the Bureau of Prisons in your area, take the initiative and request a training manual if one is not provided during your orientation.

Weber's Career Orientation

Promotion to higher levels in the corporate structure should be determined by seniority, experience, and job performance. An important goal of this characteristic is to promote loyalty to the organization.

FCI-Miami's Career Orientation   As evidenced by the organizational chart, FCI-Miami follows Weber's career orientation closely. The administrative-line middle-level employees can, through conscientious work, climb to the top of the organizational ladder, up to the position of associate warden. The warden, the associate wardens, and the executive staff positions (such as camp administrators, executive assistants, and UNICOR supervisors) are selected in a competitive selective process from a pool of qualified employees who meet the qualifications and have functioned at least at lower levels of responsibility: for example, a warden having served as an associate warden or an associate warden having served as an executive assistant or a camp administrator (Huling, 1997).

Some high-level positions in other criminal justice agencies depart from Weber's characteristic. For instance, some police chiefs and agency directors, among others, are appointed by politicians, while their subordinates are selected for promotion through civil service procedures. Promotions of other support and clerical staff are determined by qualifying examinations and recommendations by supervisors. Although they may differ, most criminal justice agencies have a method of promotion designed for career advancement.

Weber's Efficiency and Effectiveness

If an organization adheres to all the characteristics mentioned previously, it will run efficiently and effectively.

FCI-Miami's Efficiency and Effectiveness   Because of confusion in the literature regarding the terms *effectiveness* and *efficiency*, I use Hall's (1977, p. 85) conclusion that effectiveness is the extent to which an organization accomplishes its goals, while efficiency reflects the number of resources used to yield a unit of production.

On the basis of written assignments from interns, verbal reports from the warden and administrative staff, and observations during class tours and site visits to the prison, I have assumed that the organization is effective. However, the FPC has a problem with *walkaways*, inmates who walk away from the compound to obtain sex or liquor; some walkaways are apprehended on their return to the compound, and others are discovered to be missing during nonscheduled census counts before they return. These incidences are technically referred to as *escapes* for administrative purposes, but the walkaways are not prosecuted on new charges. Administrative and technical definitions may vary (Huling, 1997). Although this situation may not be viewed by the administrators as an example of ineffectiveness, it may be considered as such by the community. As an intern, do not assume that because your agency is functioning effectively, it is also functioning efficiently.

Weber's Impersonal Orientation

The working environment should be impersonal.

FCI-Miami's Impersonal Orientation   This characteristic is crucial in a prison setting because many crimes can elicit prejudice. Although most personnel are disgusted by drug pushers, child molesters, and perpetrators of other heinous crimes, a certain degree of objectivity is necessary if these inmates are to be treated fairly.

Weber's Administration of Communication

Communication is administered by written documents that move through the hierarchical levels of authority.

FCI Miami's Administration of Communication   As indicated by the organizational chart, the prison's and camp's communications move formally from the warden to the associate warden of operations and associate warden of programs, who then forwards them to the intended office and/or individual. The following is a typical routing sequence of a document from a unit. Normally, a document goes from the point of origin to the department head; to the case manager coordinator (CMC), a quality-control position; to the respective associate warden; and then to the warden (Huling, 1997). In formal structured organizations, the chain of command can be awkward because each bit of communication must pass through a higher level of management. However, in a hierarchical system, this management of communication is essential.

THE INFORMAL AGENCY STRUCTURE

During your internship, you may work in an agency that functions more casually, disregarding the Weberian model. If so, the agency would be thought of as having an informal organizational structure. This structure has been considered by organizational theorists to be more personal, realistic, and humane than the formal organizational structure because individual and group affiliations are key contributors to its development. This model also provides a sense of identity as well as personal and occupational security, which can be difficult to obtain in a bureaucracy.

During the course of the program, some interns have worked in agencies with informal organizational structures. In this section I present the characteristics of this model and explain them using as an example one of our program's agencies, the ARISE Foundation, which develops educational programs for children and adolescents. The foundation has four programs: Minicops, Envirocops, Sprouts, and Secrets of Success. The informal organizational structure of the Secrets of Success program, which provides courses in life-skills training that entertain as they educate teenagers in school classrooms, halfway houses, residential treatment facilities, and jail cells, is shown in Figure 4.3. A comparison of the formal and informal structures will reveal that the informal structure has an immense influence on communication among organizational members.

Figure 4.3   ARISE
Foundation Secrets of Success
Program Organizational
Chart: Informal
Organizational Structure

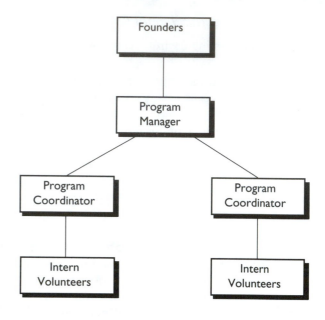

Hierarchical Model

Although the ARISE Foundation has a formal hierarchy of authority, including the founders, program manager, program coordinators, interns, and volunteers, this formal structure presents problems for completing daily assignments. Hoy and Miskel (1978) called these problems *blocks*, which means that any part of the organizational structure can influence and change the outcome of a process occurring between a subordinate and a superordinate. For example, it is the program manager's responsibility to complete and sign an intern's midterm and final evaluations (because he has a master's degree, the necessary credential for supervising interns). Frequently, the program manager is unavailable, so the program coordinator completes and forwards the evaluation by fax, explaining that the original will be sent as soon as the program manager has signed it. Thus, the informal organizational structure has come into play.

Even though many organizations attempt to function according to Weber's formal structure, during your internship experience you will find that for work to be expedited in some agencies, most employees use the informal organizational structure.

Gordon and McBride (1990) reported that the informal hierarchy in any criminal justice agency can be based upon such variables as expertise, seniority, ethnicity, blood relationships, mutual interests, and comparative upbringing.

The informal structure of the ARISE Secrets of Success program, shown in Figure 4.3, indicates that the founders are the most important people in the program, since they play the central role in policy planning. The program manager's expertise is important in the organization's informal structure. Even though the program manager performs some of the same tasks as other employees, he manages the program because he has a higher (master's) degree. Seniority plays a significant role in this organization. For example, even though a newly hired program coordinator had the experience to perform certain duties that are done by a long-time coordinator, the manager would be reluctant to transfer these duties to the new coordinator or split them between the two coordinators, so they would remain with the coordinator with seniority. The interns form a distinct group, which could be considered a clique. They are involved in hands-on activities with the teenagers, and because of the casual environment in the residential treatment facilities, most of them wear jeans and shirts instead of the usual professional attire. The volunteers participate in some activities with the teenagers and perform most of the clerical work.

Rivalries commonly occur in the informal organizational model because of the competition for resources, bonuses, and control. In the ARISE Secrets of Success program, there is a mild rivalry between the interns and the volunteers. Because some of the volunteers have been a part of the organization longer than some of the interns and have a need for control, they are not eager to relinquish some of their responsibilities, which the interns are quite capable of handling. Mutual interests also play an important role in the informal structure of this organization because some of the activities with the teenagers include life-skills training and all the trainers need to be interested in making the training successful (Jean, 1997).

Division of Labor

In the informal model, the division of labor is unclear and the job descriptions and responsibilities do not correspond with the organizational chart. During your internship, you may observe that some co-workers perform several tasks that are not in their job descriptions, perhaps because they did not initially know what was included in their job descriptions or because the agency was understaffed. The position of program coordinator at ARISE is a good example of this phenomenon. The coordinator performs several tasks when the program manager is absent that are not in the job description but have become assumed responsibilities. An intern working in a community corrections agency reported that the lines that divide each staff member's responsibilities are not always clearly drawn. Often, when one staff member is out of the office, another staff member performs that person's duties. For example, when a legal technician was on vacation from the community corrections agency, another technician's secretary performed his duties, even though they were not in her job description (Homa, 1997).

On the other hand, these overlapping responsibilities could help to prevent boredom, which is a major drawback of the division of labor. As busy as certain areas or days can be, there are times (known as *downtime*) in any organization when an employee's or intern's job can be boring. It is possible for a trainer to become bored by presenting the same materials repeatedly. And as one intern who was working in the police department reported: "There are times in a policeman's job that are downright boring.…There were instances in which for 3–4 hours we had no calls to attend to" (Gutierrez, 1997, p. 22).

During your internship, you will probably experience periods of downtime, regardless of placement. You may also encounter areas in the agency in which the assignments are monotonous but significant. For example, an intern working with the Secret Service was rotated from the Protective Service Unit, where among other exciting things, she witnessed the intricate planning of protection for a vice-presidential visit, to the Counterfeit Unit, where even though she was able to process counterfeit notes, she became bored with the repetitiveness of the process, since the field office receives from $45,000 to $125,000 in counterfeit currency weekly (Livingston, 1997).

The solution to boredom in a formal organizational structure may be for supervisors to reevaluate and rewrite job descriptions or for employees to transfer to other positions in the organization. In an informal structure, however, many employees adjust the duties to make their work more interesting. For instance, the intern who complained of the police officers' downtime stated that the officers used those 3–4 hours to get to know the community better.

Rules and Regulations

Most criminal justice organizations have rules and regulations that guide their daily operations. However, during your internship, you will discover that these rules and regulations are not always followed because the vast number of laws, state statutes, and policies that employees of criminal justice agencies must be knowledgeable about, and comply with, are so complicated. The employees of the ARISE Secrets of Success program are bound by the informal guidelines of the juvenile justice system, particularly those of the residential treatment facilities where the training takes place. In many instances, the prevailing situation will influence the discretion used by a law enforcement officer, a correctional officer, or a juvenile justice worker in enforcing a particular law, statute, or policy.

A law enforcement officer's decision to arrest someone, a correctional officer's decision to place an inmate in solitary confinement, or a juvenile justice worker's decision to revoke educational privileges all have many legal and illegal bases. A person can easily cover up his or her illegal use of authority through legal means. As a case in point, one intern reported:

> I also noticed what is referred to as a police subculture. This is characterized by secrecy and insulation from others in the society. In the case where I was a witness to a police shooting, it was clearly a situation of police bonding together to protect a fellow officer. One officer supposedly "dropped" or planted a gun after learning that the alleged offender did not ever have a gun that could have been a threat to the officer who shot him. A second officer falsified a report to justify his partner's shooting. This officer was arrested. All three officers are currently suspended with pay. (Gutierrez, 1997)

As an intern in an agency with an informal structure, you may observe that ethical rules and standards are not always followed. For instance, one staff member will prepare a report and another staff member will sign it and take credit for it. One intern reported that her agency's contract oversight specialist, who is supposed to do the projection of expenditures for the next three fiscal years, has someone else in the office prepare it; he then signs it and returns it to the central office as his own work (Homa, 1997). Although these are two good examples of how informal structures can be dysfunctional, informal organizational structures play important roles in the management of the daily business of enforcing the law in the criminal justice system.

Career Orientation

In most organizations with formal organizational structures, including criminal justice agencies, seniority and accomplishments are usually considered for promotions. This is not always the case in organizations with informal structures. For instance, an intern at a police department with an informal structure was informed that for an officer to advance to a higher level (such as sergeant or lieutenant), a specific number of years in a current position, a qualifying score on the particular examination, and an opening for the position were necessary. The intern quickly learned, however, that politics are also involved in career advancement. Often, officers who were better qualified were passed over for an officer with fewer qualifications. For example, a female patrol officer was promoted three levels (from patrol officer to lieutenant), bypassing other officers who met the criteria for advancement to that position.

It is obvious that politics played an important role in this promotion. This is not an unusual situation in criminal justice agencies because the agency officials (such as police chiefs, sheriffs, and agency directors) are elected or appointed by members of the community and engage in internal and external political activities.

Efficiency and Effectiveness

After reviewing the annual report of the ARISE Foundation's Secrets of Success program, I concluded that the organization appears to be effectively realizing its goals:

> The goal of the program is to motivate learners to get a grip on life instead of watching it slide down the tubes. It wants to be a wake-up call from bad attitudes and negative energies to empowering beliefs and new beginnings. The program is meant to focus on education, good jobs and success, rather than on crime, drugs and hanging out. The program hopes that its learners will become modern-day storytellers, as they share what they have learned with family and friends. That way, participants [can] change the world by changing themselves. ARISE hopes that those participants will become family leaders [who will] establish successful lives and careers [and] who will become mentors, storytellers, artists and healers of tomorrow. The Secret of Success program has no ending. It continues to grow, to evolve, and provide brighter futures for young adults and those whose lives they touch, turning cycles of violence into cycles of success. (Jean, 1997)

However, since I am unaware of its budgetary expenditures, I am unable to comment on its efficiency.

Impersonal Orientation

ARISE has an impersonal orientation that prevents the use of biases in dealing with juvenile delinquents. One intern reported that working in the halfway house "is like stepping into a different world and seeing people with different sets of morals and attitudes about life." Before accepting an internship in the criminal justice area, whether the agency has a formal or informal organizational structure, you must *definitely* feel that you are capable of an impersonal orientation.

Administration of Communication

In the informal organizational model, communication differs from communication in the formal model in that memorandums are sent and received on the basis of rapport, cliques, and the status of the person sending or receiving the memorandum. The ARISE Secrets of Success program provides an example of a directive that was interpreted differently by the intern and the program manager and, consequently, was not complied with by the intern, causing a bad first impression. The program manager, believing that the intern did not know the location of the halfway house where the internship would take place, gave a verbal directive to the program coordinator to notify the intern that she should meet the program manager at the ARISE office to be driven to the location. The intern informed the coordinator that she knew the location of the halfway house and would meet the manager there. The coordinator did not convey this change in plans to the manager, who waited an hour for the intern, assuming that she was not dependable and perhaps should not have the placement. The manager then called to inform me that he could not rely on the intern and would like to cancel the placement. Upon arriving at the halfway house, he discovered that the intern had been waiting there for two hours. No one at the placement phoned the main office to inquire why the manager was late (or to tell him that the intern was waiting for him there). I received a second call explaining the situation and apologizing for the first call. In the end, the intern received the highest evaluation of those who have worked in the program. Thus, this is evidence that personalities and misinterpretations must be considered in the chain of communication.

AGENCY PERSONNEL MANAGEMENT

During your internship, the main personnel management practices with which you should be concerned are *hiring, training,* and *evaluation.* Another important issue when unions represent criminal justice employees in negotiating with the management is *collective bargaining.* Although observing the process as an intern may be interesting and worthwhile, it will not apply to you.

Most interns go through the same procedures as those of new hires at various agencies, but it is still a good idea to discuss the hiring practices with your placement supervisor. For example, when you apply for an internship with the Office of the State Attorney, the Secret Service, or local police department, you may be subjected to a background check, although it may not be as extensive as if you were going to be hired by the organization. Also, many criminal justice agencies require written and physical examinations for new hires but not for interns. Furthermore, work experience and letters of recommendation are not always required when applying for an internship;

however, these factors, as well as your educational background, play an important role in obtaining employment with most criminal justice or social services agencies.

As an intern, you will receive some level of training, most of which will be informal on-the-job training guided by a supervisor or co-worker, but this training will not be as extensive as that which a newly hired employee receives. For example, while interning at a police department, your involvement will be limited to instructions in preparing minor reports and participating in ride-alongs. In contrast, police departments require formal training for employees, who must attend an academy or school, participate in supervised field training, and serve a probationary period before they become law enforcement officers.

Training is important for a number of reasons. Besides learning the practices, standards, and perspectives of fellow employees, it gives people the opportunity to become familiar with up-to-date trends in the profession. Many criminal justice agencies provide in-service training for all employees. If you are interested in obtaining employment with your internship agency, I suggest that you attend as many in-service training workshops as you are permitted.

Most organizations evaluate their employees regularly. These evaluations may be standard procedures that are highly valued by both the employees and managers in considering promotions and pay increases, or they may just be cursory and have no promotional or monetary value, as in evaluations to determine the "employee of the month." All criminal justice agencies use written evaluations to determine salary increases and promotions.

INFLUENCE OF THE PLACEMENT AGENCY ON THE INTERNSHIP

Again, the organizational model of your agency, whether formal or informal, and how well you adjust to it are two determining factors in the type of internship that you will experience. Over the years, I have had mixed reviews from my students, some favoring the formal model and some favoring the informal model. Many of the interns enjoyed the fixed rules and codes of conduct that the formal organization provided but complained that it was difficult to adjust to being left out of the informal cliques, which should not have been a concern. (Many supervisors have informed me that it is best for interns to be open-minded observers and avoid interoffice politics and cliques.) On the other hand, some interns have reported that their internships were successful and rewarding because they experienced and had to adjust to both the formal and informal structures of their agencies. It should be noted, however, that some students have been victimized by the informal organizational structure. For instance, one intern was given a low score on an evaluation because he was spending "too much" ride-along time with an officer who had filed a discrimination complaint against the intern's supervisor.

If at any time during your internship you feel uncomfortable with the organizational structure of your agency, do not hesitate to contact your supervisor or internship coordinator for assistance in making the proper adjustments. Recognizing and appreciating the formal and informal organizational structures of your agency are critical for adjusting to your workplace, your co-workers, and your agency assignments, which together guarantee a successful training experience.

SUMMARY

This chapter has provided information on the formal and informal organizational structures that are present in all organizations. Although both structures exist to some degree, in most organizations one may be more prevalent than the other. Formal organizational structures provide fixed rules and codes of conduct, as described in this chapter for the Bureau of Prison's FCI-Miami. Over the years, most interns in our program have reported that Weber's characteristic of a formal organizational structure—the hierarchical model, division of labor, rules and regulations, career orientation, efficiency and effectiveness, impersonal orientation, and communication—have been operating in their agencies. Still others have reported that although their agencies have formal organizational charts, they function more casually, with informal organizational structures. While Weber's formal model has been criticized as being impersonal, the informal structure has been considered by some theorists to be more humane. The informal model also provides a better sense of job security and personal identity. The programs of the ARISE Foundation, such as the Secrets of Success program, have been used to present the characteristics of the informal organizational model. A comparison of the formal and informal structures will reveal that the formal structure has an immense influence on communication among the organizational members.

During your internship, you need to be concerned about the hiring, training, and evaluation practices of your agency. As an intern you will probably go through the same procedures as a newly hired employee. However, it is still a good practice to discuss these procedures with your supervisor. You will discover that the background investigations and physical and written examinations are usually more extensive for a new employee than for an intern.

Whether the organizational structure of your agency is formal or informal, be aware that your ability to adjust to its model will greatly influence the success of your internship. I have received mixed reviews from my students—some enjoyed the fixed rules and codes of conduct of the formal structure, while others were more comfortable with the informal structure. In the event that you feel uncomfortable with the structure of your agency, contact your supervisor or coordinator immediately for assistance in making the necessary adjustments to guarantee a successful internship experience.

c h a p t e r   5

Pragmatic Agency Concerns

Questions for Students

What impact does bureaucracy have on your agency's performance?

How does bureaucracy affect the financial disbursements of your agency?

In what way does judicial consideration influence the efficiency of the agency's employees?

BUREAUCRACY AND CONTROL

This chapter provides insight into three systems—bureaucratic, financial, and judicial—that influence the criminal justice system and consequently, your agency. *Control* is a key word in the administration of justice. For instance, the ability to control people, evident in the way that laws are enacted and enforced, results in a pervasive bureaucratic (political) influence throughout the criminal justice system, from the police to the courts to the prisons. Those who study "critical" criminology report that the criminal justice system mirrors the values of individuals and groups with political power. This type of control may be more evident for those who intern in small communities where one family or group has control over the limited political and economic existence of the citizenry. In larger communities, however, criminal justice special-interest groups compete for the power necessary to sway their communities' judgment.

Most of you will intern for agencies in large communities where special-interest groups are constantly attempting to accomplish their goals through this bureaucratic process. According to Cox and Wade (1998), despite the negative connotations of bureaucratic corruption or any other type of exploitation of the criminal justice system for individual profit, the relationship between politics and criminal justice should not be considered negative, but "necessary and desirable in a democratic society" (p. 24). Some researchers claim that special-interest groups are beneficial in helping criminal justice practitioners become more aware and observant of the social values of the community (Bent, 1974). During your internship, you will be introduced to other important terms related to bureaucratic, financial, and judicial considerations, such as *politics, power, authority*, and *discretion*.

Politics

Lasswell (1958, p. 5) stated it very simply: "Politics is who gets what, when, and how." As an intern, you will observe criminal justice practitioners developing mutual alliances shaped by political considerations. One example is the relationship between political parties and the appointments of prosecutors, police chiefs, and judges, among others. Another example is the organization of special-interest groups by criminal justice practitioners, such as law enforcement coalitions and criminal justice task forces on corrections, which seek to influence policymaking decisions that will benefit agencies' goals. In 1986 the American Correctional Association (ACA), an organization of correctional workers, was awarded a grant by the National Institute of Corrections, U.S. Department of Justice, to develop a handbook on public correctional policies. The 21 public correctional policies were endorsed by the ACA.

During your internship, you will note that although there is an overall political influence, it may not be felt on a daily basis. In Wilson's (1968) study on the association between politics and the police, little day-to-day political influence on community policing was reported. However, the community's bureaucratic culture was significant in determining the selection of the police chief, the manner of law enforcement, and the character of departmental policy. No matter the style of bureaucracy, police departments depend on politicians for resources, such as personnel, salaries, and benefits, that are negotiated through official representatives of local residents. Chambliss (1994) observed that through their votes police officers, as community residents, can influence the results of elections and hence play a part in selecting politicians for these negotiations.

Those of you who are interning in prosecutors' offices may observe the political relationship between the police and prosecutors. Remember that prosecutors are politicians, whose election is usually supported by primary political groups, which gives them considerable discretionary powers. Police officers also exercise significant discretion in making arrests, and their relationship with prosecutors greatly influences that discretion. For example, original arrest cases are ultimately sent to the prosecutor for additional preparation. Consequently, the practices and wishes of the prosecutor influence the types of arrests the police officers make and the kinds of cases the officers submit to the prosecutor. On the other hand, even though a police officer may believe that an arrest is warranted and the case should go to court, the prosecutor, in fear of losing a difficult case and thereby losing political support, could take advantage of his or her position and discretionary powers and drop the case. Of course, this is not the norm. The need of the public, the police, and the courts to protect their vested interests usually limits the police officers' and prosecutors' use of their discretionary powers.

Politics also plays a considerable role at higher levels of the criminal justice system. The next level for the prosecutor is usually a judgeship, which is rarely attained without the support of a political party. In several states, the citizens elect county and circuit court judges, but in others, such as Florida, judges are appointed by the state governors on recommendations from nonpartisan judicial nominating commissions. Federal judges are appointed by the president with confirmation by the Senate. Baker and Meyer (1980) reported that most appointed federal judges are of the same political party as the president. An appointment to the Supreme Court is also political, as are the Court's decisions to hear cases and who will write the majority opinions (Woodward and Armstrong, 1979). Just as the corrections field has its associations, police officers have their local and national political organizations. Attorneys are represented by local and state bar associations and the American Bar Association. Two additional arms of corrections are state parole boards, whose members are politically appointed, and probation departments, whose probation officers are hired by chief justices of circuit courts or panels of judges.

Power and Authority

On the basis of Blau's (1964) discussion of politics, *power* may be defined as the ability of individuals or organizations to force their convictions repeatedly on others despite resistance, and *authority* may be defined as the appropriate use of power by people in distinctively appointed capacities.

As was shown earlier with regard to politics and power, power and authority are perplexingly intermixed. Politics, power, and authority work together when, for example, the society allows people in particular capacities the privilege of using (or misusing) specific types of power, although the bestowal of this privilege is a political process in which individuals or groups are elected to positions of authority (Cox and Wade, 1998). It is widely believed that political power and authority in the criminal justice system have been used by the wealthy against those without money, power, or authority. Several studies have reported that upper-income groups are less suspicious of the police than are lower-income groups, and that blacks of all income levels, whether African-American, Haitian, or other Caribbean islanders, distrust the police (Flowers, 1988; Kramer, 1992; Mann, 1993; Taylor et al., 1994). In addition, many writers have reported that black youths receive harsher treatment by the police than do their white counterparts (Taylor and Bing, 1995). Of course, these are issues of discretion, which are discussed below.

During your internship, observe the nature and magnitude of the connection among politics, power, and authority at your agency. This will help you appreciate the overall effect of these elements on the criminal justice system and the practitioners who operate within it, as well as the direct influence on your agency.

Discretion

Although the term *discretion* pervades the criminal justice system, there is no consensus on its meaning. Cole (1970, p. 477) broadly defined it as "the authority to make decisions without reference to specific rules or facts, using instead one's own judgment," whereas

Newman (1970, p. 479) defined it as "the authority to choose among alternative actions or of not acting at all." Some social scientists embrace Newman's definition, while others think it is useless because by contending that "all decisions are discretionary, discretion becomes merely a residual category for everything an author cannot otherwise explain" (Neubauer, 1992, p. 91). LaFave and Scott (1972) concluded that discretion derives from the lack of a precise and rational body of criminal law and the failure of state legislatures to draft precise criminal codes that specify all behavior considered criminal and omit all other behavior. As they noted, "In part the problem is the result of poor draftsmanship and a failure to revise the criminal law to eliminate obsolete provisions" (pp. 18–19). During your internship, it is important for you to be aware of the many faces of discretion: public, police, prosecutorial, defense, judicial, and correctional.

Interns working in police departments, public defenders' offices, and prosecutors' offices are introduced immediately to *public discretion* and are surprised about the significant magnitude of the discretionary powers of community residents; that is, upon observing a suspicious or criminal act, each citizen has the discretion to report or not to report it. Many studies have indicated that thousands of crimes in this country go unreported because many citizens are reluctant to exercise this discretion (Flowers, 1988; Livingston, 1996; Mann, 1993). During classroom discussions, students have described how citizens' discretion about testifying or not testifying has influenced civil and criminal cases. This same discretion is used with regard to decisions to break or abide by the law and whether to exercise one's vote for or against various law enforcement issues.

"Differential enforcement of the law" (Flowers, 1988) is another phrase used for *police discretion*. Police officers have the power to issue traffic tickets or just to reprimand drivers, to arrest or not to arrest suspects, to investigate or not to investigate crimes, to shoot or not to shoot, and so on. However, as mentioned earlier, an officer's ability to arrest and/or investigate could be jeopardized by a citizen's discretion.

Two types of law enforcement are practiced by the police: full enforcement and selective enforcement. Some police officers believe that full enforcement of the law is "seldom possible or desirable" (Cox and Wade, 1998, p. 37). The power to use personal judgment to decide to arrest a suspect or to investigate a case is essentially selective law enforcement. Because the daily actions of police officers are seldom evaluated administratively or judicially, these discretionary powers can easily turn from discretion to racism, discrimination, violence, and various other types of unlawful enforcement. Prosecutors and judges, however, have the power to reverse the decisions of police officers, except in cases of shootings, which are handled by the Internal Affairs Divisions of police departments, which oversee the behavior of police officers. Nevertheless, these first personal judgments by police officers are considered a basic discretionary power (Flowers, 1988).

Prosecutors (also called district attorneys, state's attorneys, or chief prosecutors) use *prosecutorial discretion* to prosecute or not to prosecute, which many criminal justice practitioners believe is the most powerful of all the discretionary powers. As Neubauer (1992, p. 102), stated: "The prosecutor is the most powerful official in the criminal courts." The prosecutor is considered the principal law enforcement official of the community, with the basic responsibility of protecting the public. This is regarded as the foremost position in the criminal justice system because police officers, defense attorneys, judges, and probation officers specialize in certain phases of the criminal justice procedure, whereas the prosecutor's responsibilities cross all these domains, making this the only official to work daily with all the practitioners of the criminal justice system. Those of you who are interning in the court system will have the opportunity to observe the powers of the prosecutor. These powers will become evident when the prosecutor uses his or her discretion to determine which defendants are to be prosecuted, the type of pleas to be bargained, and the severity of sentencing.

Defense attorneys share their discretionary powers with their clients. Although they may use their discretionary powers to decide whether to accept cases (private or court referred) or how much time to invest in cases, other decisions must be made with the defendants, such as what motions to file, what pleas to enter, and whether to plea-bargain. Because plea bargaining is attributed to most of the guilty pleas in the United States, some practitioners consider it a form of discretion involving the defendant, the defense attorney, the prosecutor, and occasionally, the judge. However, most people are so intimidated by the legal process that they frequently give up their discretion and allow their defense attorneys to exercise complete discretion.

Gifis (1978) reported that *correctional officials* also frequently utilize discretion through differential treatment of institutionalized criminals. Among other things, they can decide whether to ignore or report an incident to the warden. Probation and parole officers, as extensions of correctional officers, also exercise a great deal of discretion in their capacity, to decide how strictly to enforce the conditions of probation or parole, including whether to allow individuals to travel or relocate outside the state. Juvenile probation officers even have the discretion to decide whether a probationer can marry, travel or relocate, or join the armed forces (Cox and Wade, 1998). Although there is much controversy regarding the types and use of discretion, practitioners believe that the function of discretion at all levels of the criminal justice system is invaluable. During your internship, be aware of how the political process operates and the impact of bureaucracy on your agency's performance.

FINANCE AND POLITICS

Financial considerations, which are also influenced by politics, play a crucial role in agencies' acquisition and allocation of financial resources. Most criminal justice agencies are funded by tax dollars. Although some agencies receive federal funds, the majority receive local and state funds. Presently, federal assistance to local and state agencies is at an all-time low, which has forced local and state governments to seek new avenues of funding for their criminal justice agencies. In most agencies, employees' salaries and benefit packages receive the highest financial consideration. As of late, all three levels of government have been more careful and creative in managing their financial resources, particularly in the field of corrections, where the trend is toward privatizing prisons. Furthermore, "between 1987 and 1993, state spending increases for corrections outpaced higher education by 41 percent nationwide" (Walters, 1995, p. 10).

Managing the budget is the most important daily function of an agency. A budget is a strategy to determine the agency's financial management based on anticipated income. Not only is it necessary to know the daily operating expenses, it is also important to be able to project the income required for future years of operation.

An agency's budget must be prepared in either of three ways: as a line-item budget, a planned program budget, or a zero-based budget. For a *line-item budget*, each unit of the agency is designated a line and shows customary costs, which can be used to compare from one fiscal year to the next. (See Figure 5.1 for a sample of a line-item budget.) The fiscal year may not always be the regular calendar year; for example, the fiscal year for your agency may be from October to October instead of January to January as is the calendar year. A *planned program budget* is more complex; each agency area is examined in terms of designated operational goals; then the manager of each area has to justify present and future expenses based on the methods used to achieve the operational goals. (See Figure 5.2 for an example of a planned program budget.) A *zero-based budget* is even more difficult. In zero-based budgeting, a completely new budget is adapted annually. The area managers must justify all expenses and the need for the services that are rendered.

With all three types of budgets, all the managers prepare budgets for their areas or departments and send them to the agency's financial representative, who prepares submissions forms for the budgetary items. The financial representative then sends these forms to the committee of the state legislature that is responsible for budgetary matters. The committee members review and edit these budgetary items and accept the agency's budget, which is voted on by the entire legislature. If the budget is approved, expenditures are allocated, and periodic audits are conducted.

Number of Placements		782
Line Item Description	%	Total
Contract Period	07/01/96-06/30/97	
Executive Director	100.00%	65,000.00
Project Director	100.00%	36,847.00
Training Specialist	100.00%	42,015.00
Accountant	100.00%	40,488.00
Administrative Assistant	100.00%	19,575.00
Program Assistant	100.00%	18,569.00
Program Assistant	100.00%	16,391.00
Program Assistant	100.00%	13,335.50
Case Manager/Trainer	100.00%	27,300.00
Job Developer/Counselor	100.00%	27,591.00
Job Developer/Counselor	100.00%	25,500.00
Job Developer/Counselor	100.00%	24,388.00
Job Developer/Counselor	100.00%	24,157.00
Job Developer/Counselor	100.00%	23,108.00
Job Developer/Counselor	100.00%	22,854.00
Counselor (Summer Youth)	100.00%	2,666.00
Total	100.00%	429,784.50

Figure 5.1   Miami Criminal Justice Agency Line-Item Budget

		%	Total
Number of Placements			782
Line Item Description		%	Total
Contract Period		07/01/96-06/30/97	
002	Participants' Wages	100%	16,320.00
003	Participants' FICA	100%	1,248.00
004	Participants' Workcomp	100%	168.00
006	Client Transport SYETP	100%	2,297.00
101	Staff Salaries	100%	429,784.50
200	Staff MICA (Medicare)	100%	6,231.00
201	Staff FICA (Social Security)	100%	26,646.64
202	Staff Worker's Compensation	100%	6,016.98
203	Staff Unemployment	100%	3,857.00
204	Staff Group Ins.	100%	34,200.00
205	Staff Group Life Ins.	100%	1,710.00
240	Gen'l Adm. Overhead	100%	35,232.00
000	Courier Services	100%	675.00
252	Audit Cost	100%	9,500.00
301	Gen Liability Insurance	100%	2,340.00
303	Bonding	100%	588.00
304	Other Insurance (Flood)	100%	182.00
350	Telephone-Local	100%	4,920.00
350	Telephone-Long Distance	100%	1,080.00
360	Electrical Services	100%	4,992.00
410	Equipment Repair & Maintenance	100%	3,419.00
411	Bldg. Maint-Janitor	100%	3,342.00
415	Confer & Prof Meeting	100%	500.00
450	Equipment Rental(copier,computer,phone)	100%	9,533.00
460	Space Rental	100%	17,568.00
501	Postage	100%	1,200.00
502	Printing	100%	3,900.00
503	Publications Books	100%	200.00
504	Advertising	100%	250.00
507	Membership	100%	1,500.00
510	Local Travel Reimb.	100%	16,992.00
521	Office Supplies	100%	4,355.00
522	Special Client Supplies	100%	5,872.00
527	Supportive Service	100%	5,400.00
530	Client Services	100%	2,525.00
542	Tuition & Books	100%	6,046.00
600	OJT Wages (Participants)	100%	8,800.00
TOTAL		100%	679,481.00

Figure 5.1   (cont'd)

Department of Corrections
Budget Summary
(FY1995-96)

TOTAL APPROVED BUDGET:	$ 1,617,612,842
OPERATING FUNDS	
Expenditures by Budget Entity:	
Office of the Secretary and Office of Management and Budget	$ 19,081,078
Office of Programs	$ 5,949,721
Health Services	$ 194,593,820
Correctional Education School Authority	$ 15,795,422
Office of Operations and Regional Administration	$ 5,401,141
Major Institutions	$ 812,695,807
Probation and Parole Services	$ 195,273,144
Community Facilities and Road Prisons	$ 30,160,974
Youthful Offender- Assistant Secretary's Office	$ 540,559
Youthful Offender- Institutions	$ 40,663,980
TOTAL OPERATING FUNDS	$ 1,320,155,646
FIXED CAPITAL OUTLAY FUNDS	
EXPENDITURES BY PROJECT CLASSIFICATION:	
To provide additional capacity through expansion & new construction	$ 90,224,153
To maintain existing facilities & meet requirements of regulatory agencies	$ 9,826,422
TOTAL FIXED CAPITAL OUTLAY FUNDS	$ 100,050,575
LOCAL FUNDS	
VOLUME OF COLLECTION ACTIVITIES:	
Cost of Supervision Fees	$ 21,845,024
Restitution and Court-Ordered Payments	$ 38,667,264
Subsistence and Transportation Fees	$ 8,144,158
INMATE BANKING ACTIVITIES:	
Total Deposits	$ 59,584,499
Total Disbursements	$ 59,233,509
June 30, 1996 Total Assets	$ 5,056,204
INMATE WELFARE FUND ACTIVITY:	
Merchandise Sales	$ 30,707,685
Gross Profit From Sales	$ 7,075,199
Inmate Telephone Commissions	$ 12,942,025
June 30, 1996 Retained Earnings	$ 13,367,787

Florida Department of Corrections*1995–96 Annual Report

Figure 5.2   Sample Planned Program Budget

The line-item budget is popular in criminal justice agencies. The budget shown in Figure 5.1 is a line-item budget for a Miami agency whose main mission is to assist ex-convicts in their transition from prison to society. Because there is no explanation of expenditures, it is considered an open-ended budget in that the agency director is requesting funds for services performed or needed with no justification. The budget shown in Figure 5.2 is a planned program budget for the Florida Department of Corrections. With this type of budget, each service is measured and justified.

During your internship, it may or may not become obvious to you that your agency is constantly confronted with monetary and budgeting issues. After observing the situation for a while, ask your supervisor to give you some insight into the agency's budget and the effects of bureaucracy on the agency's acquisition and allocation of funds. Whereas several of my interns have been employed by agencies after interning, others could not be hired because of "freezes" on hiring owing to reduced federal or state funding to these agencies. All these issues will become clearer once you understand the type of budget under which your agency is operating.

THE AGENCY'S CONSTITUTIONAL JUSTIFICATION

Just as you should be informed about your agency's budget, you should also be aware of the constitutional justification for your agency. At the beginning of your internship, it is appropriate to request a copy of the agency's mission statement and laws that are applicable to implementing the mission. As is discussed in criminal justice courses, the legal bases for all criminal justice agencies can be found in various laws and statutes, as well as in recent court rulings and executive decisions by the three levels of government. (See Box 5.1 for the constitutional justification for the redirection of Florida's Juvenile Justice System and Box 5.2 for information on the department's vision, mission statement, and priorities.) All criminal justice agencies have a legal basis, even if they operate in the private sector, such as the organization mentioned in Figure 5.1. All law enforcement agencies; local and state courts; and county sheriffs', district attorneys', and justices of the peace officers are constitutionally authorized agencies. Many state constitutions also allow communities to establish local law enforcement agencies and courts if they are deemed necessary.

Mandated laws at all levels of government grant constitutional justification for the establishment of most criminal justice agencies and for the reorganization and redirection of various agencies and programs. A case in point is the recent revamping of Florida's juvenile justice system.

Prior to 1994 the Department of Juvenile Justice was under the auspices of the Florida Department of Health and Rehabilitative Services (HRS), a social service organization. Under the direction of HRS, the juvenile justice system was constantly under attack by the public and the media. In 1989 a task force was formed to examine and evaluate programs in other states, in 1990 the task force's recommendations were accepted, and in 1994 House Bill 1927 was passed, creating a new director of juvenile justice in the state of Florida. This is a good example of legislative powers at work and proof of the constitutional justification of this system (Florida Department of Corrections, 1995–1996).

During classroom discussions, my students have found the historical reviews (which are necessary for their term papers) of their agencies fascinating. Although they were familiar with several of the internship agencies and knew that all were established for particular reasons, they were surprised to learn that the present function of

Box 5.1   HISTORICAL OVERVIEW OF FLORIDA'S JUVENILE JUSTICE SYSTEM

Juvenile Justice Reform Act of 1990

In 1989, the Florida legislature created the Juvenile Justice System Review Task Force to review Florida's juvenile justice system and to study innovative and successful programs in other states. The task force's recommendations were later adopted in the Juvenile Justice Reform Act of 1990.

The Juvenile Justice Reform Act emphasized prevention, diversion, and early intervention programs for both delinquent and dependent children. The act funded alcohol, drug abuse, and mental health beds for juveniles. The reform act also called for reduced juvenile justice caseloads and increased use of innovative alternatives to secure detention. Community-based commitment programs were to be expanded so that juvenile offenders could be served near their home communities.

Implementing the reform act cost over $100 million. The initial appropriation was $52 million for more than 1000 juvenile offender commitment beds, nearly 400 drug abuse and mental health beds, and 500 delinquency case managers. A series of download trends in Florida's economy greatly reduced the funding available. As a result, the rush to bring new resources on line slowed dramatically while the commitment waiting list grew.

House Bill of 1927

Dissatisfied with the lack of progress in the system, the 1993 legislature chose to make sweeping changes in the organization of juvenile justice responsibilities in Florida. House Bill 1927, signed by Governor Lawton Chiles in May 1993, established Juvenile Justice as a separate operational division within the Florida Department of Health and Rehabilitative Services (HRS).

The bill strengthened the capacity and diversity of juvenile justice programs. It allocated nearly $67 miilion to help fund effective remedial services. A Deputy Secretary for Juvenile Justice was created with direct line authority over 15 new juvenile justice managers located in the HRS service districts. The purpose of direct line authority was to streamline juvenile justice decisions and increase accountability. Local accountability was enhanced by the creation of juvenile justice county councils and district boards. The volunteers on the councils and boards were charged with assessing community needs, evaluating existing services, and planning and making recommendations for the improvement of the juvenile justice continuum in their area. Many improvements followed, including:

- An increase in funding for juvenile justice by 26 percent in fiscal year 1993–1994 (total budget $252 million) and by nearly 50 percent in fiscal year 1994–95 (total budget $382 million)

- An increase in the total capacity of commitment programs and aftercare programs, which nearly doubled

---

Box 5.1 (cont'd)

- The approval of Community Juvenile Justice Partnership Grants to fund local programs for delinquency and truancy prevention, alternatives to school suspension and school safety projects
- The establishment of juvenile justice county councils and district juvenile justice boards involving representatives from law enforcement, judiciary, schools, local government, social services agencies, parents, private providers, and interested citizens

Juvenile Justice Act of 1994 and a New Direction for Juvenile Justice

The Juvenile Justice Act of 1994 created the new Florida Department of Juvenile Justice on October 1, 1994 and removed the responsibilities for juvenile justice from HRS. Governor Chiles appointed Calvin Ross to serve as secretary of the department. Secretary Ross is charged with the planning and management of programs for Children-in-Need-of-Services (CINS) and Families-in-Need-of-Services (FINS); prevention, early intervention, and diversion programs; community supervision services; detention centers; community-based-commitment programs; and other delinquency institutions and facilities. In addition, the act provided funding for each of these juvenile justice service areas.

---

many of these has changed over the years. For example, the Secret Service, which is thought of mainly as a protection service for the president, his staff, and other domestic and foreign dignitaries, was founded 1865 to protect U.S. interest in the integrity of its currency; in other words, counterfeiting was of great concern then, as it is today. However, the responsibilities of the Secret Service have increased tremendously over the years.

Other federal organizations, such as the Federal Bureau of Investigation and the Bureau of Alcohol, Tobacco, and Firearms, were established by acts of Congress. In the event that your agency supervisor and other staff members are not aware of the judicial acts relative to the agency (which some of my students have found to be the case), you may want to do this research on your own.

OVERSEEING FIELD PLACEMENTS

How are organizations and their employees made accountable for protecting the liberties of the public? In addition to politics and laws discussed previously, there is added protection from citizens themselves, the media, and the civil liberties organizations.

There is no question about the power of the people, as addressed in the section on discretion. With the advent of new technology, especially the Internet, it is more convenient for the general public to be more readily informed regarding local and national cover-ups, as well as other issues related to the criminal justice system. The

Box 5.2   FLORIDA DEPARTMENT OF JUVENILE JUSTICE

Vision

The Department of Juvenile Justice envisions a safer Florida where people experience the benefits of life resulting from the reduced risk of harm caused by juvenile delinquency.

Mission

The mission of the Department of Juvenile Justice is to provide a full range of programs and services to prevent and reduce juvenile delinquency in partnership with families, schools, communities, businesses, law enforcement, and other agencies. We are committed to a balanced approach that increases public safety, provides department and offender accountability, and affords opportunities for youths to develop into responsible citizens. To attain this balanced approach, the department addresses three priority issues in the Agency Strategic Plan: 1996–2001.

Priority Issues

1. Increase public safety by reducing the per capita number of crimes committed by juveniles through (a) improving the effectiveness and increasing the number of outcome-based delinquency prevention and early intervention programs for at-risk youths, and (b) providing for appropriate and effective levels of detention and commitment programs and services.

2. Promote local government and community involvement by creating partnerships focused on delivering juvenile justice programs and services specific to district needs and increasing public awareness of the department's mission.

3. Build accountability, effectiveness, and efficiency measures into the juvenile justice system through promoting (a) program and services quality assurance; (b) technological enhancement; (c) qualified workforce; (d) culturally competent and gender- and racially-equitable programs, services, and administrative practices; and (e) conservation of tax dollars.

media, both print and electronic, certainly provide more news information services. If one chooses to become personally involved, one only has to tune in to CNN, FOX, or MSNBC, among others news programs, for constant minute-by-minute news coverage and opportunities. Newspapers and magazines certainly also play an enormous role in policing criminal justice agencies and the conduct of their employees. Since the Civil Rights Act of 1964, numerous lawsuits have been filed over discrimination, brutality, and negligence by administrative officials. All these external checks are crucial to protecting the rights of all members of society.

SUMMARY

In this chapter we discussed the bureaucratic, financial, and judicial systems that affect your agency's performance. For interns in agencies in small communities, politics will play a different role than it will for interns in agencies located in large communities. Whereas the politics of small communities are controlled by families or groups, the politics of large communities are controlled by criminal justice special-interest groups. Bureaucracy, power, and authority are explicitly linked with the financial strategies of the agency. You may be able to witness this interaction at your internship placement by observing political alliances between your agency administrators and other criminal justice officials.

In reviewing the impact of the judicial system on your agency's operations, we introduced the authority associated with the power of discretion afforded the police, prosecutors, defense attorneys, judges, correctional officers, and the public (regarding citizens' decisions of whether to aid these officials in performing their duties).

As has been shown, it is crucial for agencies to be cost-effective and otherwise to take monetary issues into consideration if they are to be allotted their necessary fiscal resources. State tax dollars support most criminal justice agencies, although some agencies, on occasion, obtain federal assistance. Management of the budget is considered the most significant daily operation of the agency. Although budgets are prepared either by line-item, planned program, or zero-based budgeting, criminal justice agencies mainly use line-item budgeting. Therefore, you should become familiar with this type of budget.

In addition, at the beginning of your internship, you should inquire about the constitutional justification of your agency. The legal basis for most criminal justice agencies can be found in various laws and statutes, recent court rulings, and executive decisions made by local, state, or federal governments. Again, you may want to research the statutory laws related to your agency. The chapter concluded with a discussion of the parts that citizens, the media, and civil liberty organizations play in ensuring that the public's liberty is protected.

chapter 6

Agency Goals and Social System Affiliations

Questions for Students

What are the differences between your agency's official and operative goals?

How does your agency measure the effectiveness of its goals?

What are your agency's social system goals?

STATED OPERATIVE GOALS

An understanding of your agency's behavior requires a close examination of the goals indicated in its operating procedures. This chapter provides information that will help you to understand the various types of organizational goals that are important to the daily functioning of an agency.

The major categories of organizational goals that are usually discussed are official and operative goals. According to Perrow (1961), *official goals* are the general purposes of the organization, as declared by its charter, mission statement, and bureaucratic pronouncements, whereas *operative goals* are the policies that determine the actual behavior of the organization. The operative goals, standards by which daily decisions are made by agency personnel, are more relevant to understanding organizational behavior and may be different from the official goals. For example, the official goal of a police department may be to create a secure environment in the community that will enhance the quality of the citizens' lives. The official goal of the Department of Corrections may be to provide programs and services to offenders and to supervise offenders at the level of security comparable with the danger they present. These official goals are ambiguous, and as Perrow (1961) stated, they do not reflect the operative goals of political groups in organizations, decision making and competition among these groups, and the accessibility of resources.

The purpose of the goals of criminal justice agencies is to specify procedures for daily management. As discussed in Chapter 5, the establishment of agencies' official and operative goals is influenced by political, financial, and judicial considerations. An agency's traditional precedent, for example, its mission (the agency has always rendered a specific service), may also be an influence.

For organizations that are sponsored by governmental agencies, such as juvenile and adult corrections agencies, the authority for setting official goals, rules, and regulations and the procurement of capital and operating expenses lies with governmental officials appointed by political committees. The enormity of the organizations, the complicated procedures for accountability, and the pressures associated with the tenuous relationship with the political committees indicate the importance of the administrative functions. Professional influence is also increasing in these organizations, and professional groups are beginning to make a considerable impact on some components of the criminal justice system. These professionals may assume control of various organizations or may be instrumental in hiring administrators who are committed to achieving the organizations' positive goals, such as the rehabilitation of clients, as has occurred in a few federal penal institutions (privatization) and a few state juvenile correctional institutions (boot camps). These are good examples of the influence of operative goals.

The Federal Bureau of Prisons has six official goals for 1995 and beyond. It will do the following:

1. Proactively manage its offender population to ensure safe and secure operations.

2. Have a competent and representative workforce meeting the organization's needs up to and beyond the year 2000.

3. Maintain its facilities in operationally sound condition and in compliance with security, safety, and environmental requirements.

4. Manage its operation and resources in a competent and effective manner which encourages creativity and innovation in development of exemplary programs as well as excellence in maintaining the basics of correctional management. The bureau continually strives toward improvements in its effective use of resources and its efficient delivery of services.

5. Provide services and programs to address inmate needs, providing productive use-of-time activities, and facilitating the successful reintegration of inmates into society, consistent with community expectations and standards.

6. Continue to seek opportunities for expanding the involvement of community, and local, state, and federal agencies. (U.S. Department of Justice, 1995, pp. 1–12).

These are the official goals for the Bureau of Prisons provided by the U.S. Department of Justice. However, an intern working with the Bureau of Prisons reported that several operative goals have been established at her office to realize the bureau's official goals:

- Secure a new contract for a halfway house with the capacity to house 75 inmates.
- Update the computer system to enhance productivity.
- Remodel the third floor to provide office space for the community corrections administrator.
- Recruit new interns to assist in the daily operations of the office.

Are these operational goals reflective of the agency's official goals? Generally, they are. Are those of you who are presently interning aware of the official goals of your agencies? Have you been able to observe any significant difference between official and operative goals? For those of you who are just starting your internships, it is recommended that you request a copy of your agencies' official goals; inquire how, why, and by whom these particular goals were established; and note the difference between how these two sets of goals are operationalized.

During your internship, you may discover that the organization's official goals are not considered in the operative goals or that the official goals have been completely altered, a phenomenon called *goal displacement* (Gordon and McBride, 1990). Although goal displacement occurs in several criminal justice agencies, it is nearly impossible for it to occur in others.

A good example of goal displacement occurred in an agency of which I am a board member. The original official goals were to assist adult inmates in the transition from prison into society. Over the years, federal funding diminished in this area; thus, in 1996, the agency began to consider extending its services to juveniles. Today, the agency provides services to both adults and youthful offenders. In this case, goal displacement enabled the agency to maintain its organizational structure, acquire fiscal resources, preserve its public image, and retain its staff. Not only was the agency rescued by changing its official goals, but it was able to extend its scope and make an even greater contribution to the community.

The following are accounts from two interns who reported that it is impossible for goal displacement to occur in their internship agencies. The first intern reported:

> At the Federal Bureau of Prisons our goals are dictated by statute....We have a distinct mission and are held accountable for everything we do....There is no room to be creative and develop our own plans;...the Government Accounting Office looks at all our expenditures, and we must spend our money in designated areas. (Bankston, 1997)

The other intern stated:

> The goals of the Guardian Ad Litem program revolve around the power of the lay guardians (GALs). All staff members are present to assist the lay guardians by informing them when and how to "obtain information and advocate for services." The staff members organize information, upgrade organizational capabilities, and monitor legislative efforts for the sole purpose of facilitating the objectives of the GALS. The GALS

accept a case and are committed to fulfilling several official goals, with the support and supervision of the staff. These goals include: (1) to complete an intensive investigation of the case, (2) to report findings to the court, (3) to ensure representation of the children's best interests, (4) to monitor all proceedings and services relevant to the case, (5) to attend training, (6) to consult regularly with the supervisor in the particular division, (7) to participate in evaluations of your performance, and (8) to strive to attain permanency for the children at the earliest possible time. Operative goals of this agency fit these official goals well. That is, there is a very small discrepancy between the pursuit of these goals. Official goals are rigorously applied to everyday endeavors. (Santos, 1997)

Over the years, the interns in our program have asked to be placed in agencies whose work relates to their professional goals. It was also important to them that these agencies were not practicing goal displacement, which could prevent them from gaining experience in the types of agencies with the types of clients with whom they needed to work to accomplish their goals. For example, if an intern who wanted to work only with adults was placed in the agency described earlier (the coordinator being unaware of the goal displacement) and was required to work with juvenile delinquents, the experience could be unsatisfactory. If you are placed in an agency that is experiencing goal displacement and thus will be prevented from gaining experience in your chosen area, contact your coordinator as soon as possible and ask to be placed in another agency. This is not to imply that it is not good to work at an agency that is experiencing goal displacement; goal displacement is common in certain criminal justice agencies for various reasons, including those just stated. Interning at such an agency will be a problem for you only if it prevents you from receiving the experience you desire.

SOCIAL SYSTEMS GOALS

Social systems goals are related to an agency's contribution to the operation of a social system in which it is embedded (Perrow, 1961). For example, alternative schools for children who have been adjudicated delinquents by the juvenile courts are part of the school system. Organizations may perform accommodating, gratificatory, integrated, or model-maintenance functions (Parsons, 1956). For instance, Scott's (1959) study of prisons and mental hospitals reported that organizations serving integrative functions for the community will emphasize integrative functions in the organizations with which they are affiliated.

All four functions are considered important for an organization's survival, although they may be accomplished through different goals in different organizations. For example, the official goal of a police department may be to enforce laws, prevent crime, maintain order, and maintain positive police–community relations, whereas a criminal justice agency may include these four functions in its goals of providing institutional services (interviewing soon-to-be released inmates), services to clients (providing employment upon release), maintaining a professionally trained and managed organization, and proactively seeking ways to prevent recidivism by educating employers to accept and train ex-offenders.

AFFILIATIONS WITH AGENCY SYSTEMS

As earlier stated, most criminal justice agencies use a multisystems approach to accomplish their goals. Many agencies must be prepared to intervene with clients at a variety of systems levels, including individual, family, extended family, church, community, and social services. It would be impossible to describe this immensely complicated multisystem in a sketch of one organization because of the vast number and combinations of procedures in various parts of the country. Therefore, in this section a small-scale agency relationship chart for the Homestead Police Department is presented (see Figure 6.1), in addition to a description of the department's affiliations with other organizations.

The Homestead Police Department enforces federal and state laws in five patrol zones within a 13-square-mile area. The department's 72 officers provide assistance to approximately 27,000 residents. As indicated in Figure 6.1, the major social and educational agencies with which the police department is affiliated on a regular basis are the Department of Children and Family Services (CFS), Dade County Public Schools, Dade County Housing and Urban Development (HUD) Corporation, and other community programs. For example, one program, Project Start Off Smart (SOS), is a partnership program between the Homestead Police Department, Dade County Public Schools, and the CFS. The goal of SOS, created in 1991, is to stabilize the family unit, with the hope of reducing the number of interventions and eliminating the duplication of services by some agencies. Referrals to the program are provided by police officers, school personnel, CFS, and the community. In 1995, the majority of the referrals (43 percent) were for domestic violence; the remainder were for child

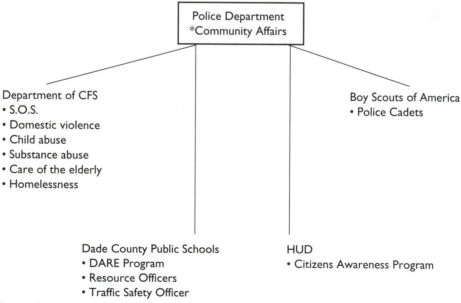

Figure 6.1   Homestead Police Department and Agency Affiliations

abuse and neglect and sexual abuse (30 percent), family services (AFDC, child custody and substance abuse) (20 percent), and miscellaneous (such as services for the elderly and homeless persons) (7 percent).

The Drug Abuse Resistance Education (DARE) Program is an affiliation between the Homestead Police Department and the Dade County Public Schools. Police officers teach the program in two area elementary schools and take students on picnics and on bowling and swimming outings. Another affiliation involves two school resource officers, one who is assigned to one area middle school and the other who divides his time between the second area middle school and the senior high schools. These officers manage the Crossover Program, which is designed for students who are at risk of dropping out who are referred to the program by the juvenile court, the Juvenile Alternative Sanctioned System, Project SOS, CFS, and school administrators or by parents' requests. The goal of DARE is to reduce school truancy, dropout, and juvenile delinquency. A third affiliation between the police department and the schools is the Traffic Safety Officer Program, in which a police officer teaches youth occupant protection and awareness of "driving under the influence" (DUI) in all Homestead schools, from kindergarten through grade 12. The Youth Occupant Protection Program's curriculum consists of information on the leading causes of death and injury to young people from automobile and bicycle accidents.

In 1995, a short-term affiliation between the police department and HUD resulted in the Citizen Awareness Program, which introduced citizens to a wide range of crime-fighting techniques, from first aid to crime reporting. The program included 11 weeks of classroom training by visiting instructors and concluded with a field trip to the police station.

One community program, the Police Explorers, is provided by the Homestead Police Department in conjunction with the Boy Scouts of America for boys aged 14 to 21. These participants, called cadets, must complete an extensive training program in a curriculum that incorporates accepted police academy requirements. Upon graduation, these Police Explorers assist patrol officers at parades and other significant activities with crowd and traffic control. Some former Police Explorers have become certified police officers, and others are currently working in a civilian capacity for the Homestead Police Department (Homestead Police Department, 1995).

Along with these social and educational affiliations, the Homestead Police Department has the same systematic relationships with criminal justice agencies for the prosecution of criminal cases as do other police departments. These agencies include the State Police, the Sheriff's Department, and those discussed earlier in Chapter 5: the Office of the State Attorney, the Public Defender's Office, the courts, the departments of probation and parole, and corrections agencies.

Although the relationships between criminal justice agencies and the Police Department are not shown in Figure 6.1, it is still evident that the multisystems are intricate for a relatively small neighborhood such as Homestead and that the department's affiliations with schools, social service agencies, and other community agencies are numerous. During your internship, you may discover that the relationships between your agency and others are different, as in the following example of a student's report of her agency's interaction with other agencies:

The Family Intervention Specialty Program's (FISP) [a division of the Florida Department of Juvenile Justice] major problem is that FISP is forced to interact with many different organizations throughout the course of one day. Each of these organizations has its own rules and regulations. The problem is that the network that integrates the separate components of the criminal justice system is so fragmented that information does not flow smoothly. For instance, at FISP we have to contact a public school for information on a client. Then we may have to pull someone's records from the courts or from the police department. More often than not, the client lives in the Liberty Square Housing Project [so] HUD gets involved. If the family needs or is already receiving some sort of benefits, we usually have to contact CFS.

Since our clients are "at risk," we deal with a lot of the alternative schools in the area. The structure of some of these schools is so littered with red tape that the schools are worse than some of the public schools. FISP must deal with all these organizations on a day-to-day basis and must also deal with the Department of Juvenile Justice. Because of time constraints, dealing with all these organizations in one day is a tremendous task in itself. Then there is the added fact that several of these organizations seem to have a problem surrendering information to anyone outside their organizations. (Henderson, 1995)

This and other problems caused the intern to become cynical about the relationship of her internship agency and other agencies. One situation that was especially upsetting to her was the replacement of FISP's official policy and initial mission, when founded in 1993, of rehabilitating youths and shielding them from the traumatic and stigmatizing experience of criminal court with the goals of 1995 legislation to "lock up young offenders and get tough on crime," which, she believed, has caused the program to be ineffective because it is operating under a philosophy for which it was not intended.

During your internship it is important to be aware that your perspective on particular criminal justice matters may be influenced by your agency's environment and to understand that other agencies' goals and responsibilities may be different. The affiliations will vary depending on the type of agency you are working in, the type of agencies that interact with your agency, and the contribution your agency wishes to make to the social system in which it is cradled.

SUMMARY

In this chapter we discussed agencies' goals and affiliations with social systems. It started by describing the difference between official and operative goals that function as rules and regulations for daily management and long-term strategies for most criminal justice organizations. It then pointed out that goal displacement is also associated with an agency's official and operative goals and can occur whenever the official goals are ignored or changed. Because most agencies work in partnership with other agencies, it is also important for them to develop social systems goals that will result in the provision of the best possible services for the community. The chapter ended with a discussion of agency affiliations in the criminal justice system. These relationships are often influenced by legal, economic, or political factors that result in administrative decisions that influence official and/or operative goals and may ultimately cause you or other agency personnel to become biased about the agency's role and affiliations with other organizations. In conclusion, in the criminal justice system, the community is always considered in the development of organizational goals, whether official or operational, and goal setting is considered an interactive process.

P A R T   I I I ———————————————————————

Field-Placement Considerations

═══

Now that you have selected your internship site, had your interview, and passed your background screening, it is time to consider what your role will be at your field placement. Your first consideration should be the available learning opportunities. Although your internship coordinator may have discussed these opportunities with you prior to placement, it is essential for you to be clear about what the agency supervisor expects of you. It is also important for the agency supervisor to be aware of what you expect to learn from your field education. No matter how exciting the placement may sound (like the Secret Service), the lack of interesting and challenging educational opportunities can result in a negative experience. It is important that you are not used as a gofer or file clerk, and it is your responsibility to clarify your role from the beginning. As an internship coordinator, I attempt to prevent or counteract any disappointments by discussing these issues before students are assigned to agencies and during site visits and by including them in the agency agreements.

Once the goals of the internship are clarified, you will begin learning by observing. It is your agency supervisor's responsibility to give you the opportunity to observe various components of the activities that occur in the agency—from clerical work to staff meetings to interactions with clients and any other pertinent services. Certainly, every element of an organization is not rewarding or fascinating, but you should be exposed to the boring as well as the exciting aspects of the placement.

On the basis of your training, once your agency supervisor thinks you are capable, you may move from observation to interaction. While your goals should include pursuing new challenges head on and considering your capabilities, your involvement in agency activities should still be closely supervised. For instance, if you have been a participant-observer in a courtroom for several weeks, your supervising attorney may allow you to try your hand at writing or helping to write legal briefs. Or, if you have observed a therapy group for several weeks, you may be asked to co-facilitate it, as well as to record your observations. Finally, you should ask your agency supervisor to give you specific information regarding the agency's policies, rules, and regulations and base your conduct and actions on them. In Chapter 7 we discuss your role as an intern. Chapter 8 will enhance your understanding of the role your agency and agency supervisor play in your internship experience. Chapter 9 will provide the same for the faculty internship coordinator, and in Chapter 10 we explain ethical standards for criminal justice professionals.

c h a p t e r   7

The Intern's Role

Questions for Students

How do you see your role as
an intern?

Do you have good
observational and writing
skills?

Are you comfortable asking
questions?

ORIENTATION

The agency staff will have been informed of your day of arrival and will have established a working assignment. In initially addressing your role as an intern, your agency supervisor's discussion of personnel practices may well include working hours, work breaks (if any), personal conduct, procedures and routines, appropriate dress (if not discussed during the interview), confidentiality of information, and any other pertinent information.

Suelzle and Borzak (1981) suggested that the roles of interns change as interns progress through a series of stages. According to these researchers, the orientation process takes place during the intern's "initial entry" stage. In this stage you will probably be both excited and anxious about the internship. The question of acceptance will be utmost in your mind.

After the orientation period, you will no longer be treated as a visitor. Your role as an intern will fall somewhere between that of a student and a professional. There will still be many tasks for you to learn, but you may also be perceived as a knowledgeable person with some skills. Keep in mind that most agencies and staff view the internship as a means of contributing to the development of young professionals, showing an ongoing commitment to the development of the profession, obtaining new input from students, providing the enriching experience of supervision to senior staff, and gaining local and national recognition.

Upon considering your experience and training, your agency supervisor may gradually increase your responsibilities. You may be encouraged to observe situations and attend staff meetings that only agency personnel usually attend. During such meetings and observations, some agency personnel may accept you and be friendly toward you, but others may not. The ambivalence they exhibit reflects their confusion about who you are and the purpose of your internship. Furthermore, the invitation to attend these functions by no means implies that your position is equal to that of a staff person, only that you are being permitted to observe another facet of the agency's operations.

The staff's reactions to you may depend a great deal on the precedents set by previous interns and whether the staff sees you as a threat. They will probably compare you to previous interns. Interns who have created a positive impression will have left high standards for you to emulate, whereas those who did not will have created a negative impression for you to counteract. During this phase, which is referred to as *probationary*, you may sometimes be judged by unfair standards that have nothing to do with your abilities and over which you have no control. However, you do have control over your ultimate evaluation, after *your* performance has been evaluated. Throughout this period, you should follow two easy rules: (1) Be honest with yourself and with others, and (2) do your best (Baird, 1996, p. 19). Remember that as a student intern, your goal is to learn. Do not be afraid to ask questions or to say you do not know an answer to a question. The best way to reduce pressure and help yourself do your best is to be honest about your limitations. This attitude will also guarantee that you have a much more fulfilling and inspiring internship.

Participant Observation

The moment you walk into the agency, the observation process begins. You immediately begin to study your surroundings, including the people and the activities that are occurring. In the agency you will be much more aware of this process than you are in other areas of your life, including the classroom, because your new responsibilities will make you more conscious of your observational role.

This type of observation requires more skills because you eventually have to record and report what you have seen and done. In most internship courses, as in mine, you are required to write an observation/participation paper that you submit at the end of the internship. Your observations in the agency will afford you the opportunity to enhance your mental note-taking skills until such time as you are able to record the significant events of each day. To keep track of these events and activities, it is helpful for you to maintain a journal, since experience in recording will help you hone the skills you need to describe and assess your internship experience. Although you may initially record everything, you will eventually need to distinguish what is important from what is insignificant. In some organizations you may be assigned to various departments for short periods to give you an idea of all their functions. My students who intern at the Secret Service, for example, spend some time in protection (guarding the president and other prominent dignitaries), some time in detecting counterfeit money, and some time in other areas. Students interning with the Office of the State Attorney must choose between working as law clerks, domestic abuse case interviewers, criminal intake counselors, or victim/witness advocates. In such cases, you ultimately have to decide which facet of the organization you want to observe in depth and ask to be assigned to that department. You will probably pay more attention to an area that is compatible with the goals you and your supervisor have determined and that are influenced by the job or jobs you actually perform at your placement.

Once you have decided in which area you are interested, you will be ready to document your daily or weekly experiences.

DATA COLLECTION METHODS

There are several ways to collect data. As I just mentioned, I encourage you to do so by keeping a journal. Entering your thoughts and impressions each day will not only ensure that the information is accurate and up to date, but it will give you valuable experience that will enhance your sense of self-reflection and note-taking skills. The following is an example of a journal entry:

Thursday, April 10, 1997

11:00–12:30

Met with Ms. Ferrell (supervisor) and followed up on yesterday's implementation of improvement priorities program. Agreed that Goal 1, readiness to start class, was achieved. We will discuss a time line for implementing Goal 2 during tomorrow's meeting. Also spoke with Joy regarding transportation to her juvenile court hearing next Tuesday. Received permission to accompany Joy to court. Will report back to Ms. Ferrel regarding the disposition of the hearing during staff meeting on Friday.

12:30–1:00

Lunch in the cafeteria. Was introduced to two students who were experiencing their first day in an alternative school setting. They both were nervous and were looking forward to the end of the school day.

1:00–2:00

Provided tutoring for two new students. Both students seemed to enjoy the special attention for a brief period and then became very distracted. Discussed situation with supervisor and submitted a brief report for the students' records.

The journal should be used to record your daily experiences at your placement. In these journal entries it is beneficial to include your personal reactions to situations, thoughts about staff or clients, and impressions of procedures or treatments and the formal or informal atmosphere of the organization. Take notes on ideas and projects that pique your curiosity so that you can discuss them with your agency supervisor at a later time. It is essential that you maintain confidentiality when you write or discuss any entry by using fictitious names or only first names when referring to clients. A chronological format, in which you indicate the day, date, and hour of activities or events; information on clients; activities; and staff involvement will be beneficial for updating your internship coordinator on your daily activities; reporting the hours you spent at the agency; and when applicable, preparing your term paper.

Starting a Journal

To record your initial impressions of the agency and its personnel, you need to decide which recording method you want to use before you begin the internship. Your first impressions of your placement are important because the first day is the only time you will be able to view the agency as a member of the community rather than as part of the organization. Furthermore, these initial impressions will come in handy when you compare them to what you have learned at the end of the placement.

Although you will eventually decide the specific areas you want to record, it is not necessary to do so during the first week. Relax and record your observations at random, without any particular focus. Later, when you are more at ease with your surroundings and the staff members, you will become aware of your specific areas of interest.

The first things you may want to include, which some of my students have done, are descriptions of the environment and whether the structure is formal or informal. Then you may want to add demographic information on the agency personnel (their ages, racial and ethnic backgrounds, and genders) and alliances (cliques) among the staff. You may want to include information on agency space allocation, the arrangement of furniture in the reception areas and offices, and how the walls are decorated. You may want to add information on how the staff dress (such as casual or business attire). Finally, you may want to include how the agency staff relate to clients, how clients respond to staff, and your impression of the relationship between the agency and the community.

When your placement environment becomes more comfortable and your observations are more perceptive, it is a good idea to begin to compare classroom theory with actual practice. During this process you may find that you either refine or reject your initial ideas and concepts on the basis of your experience in the agency.

Planning Interviews

In collecting data and recording observations for the required term paper, my students interview staff members and clients (when appropriate) to help them understand better the key issues and problems associated with the agency. Before you schedule interviews with staff and clients, you should have a good idea what your focus will be in collecting and recording this information. In my opinion, recording your interviews is the best way to analyze various people's viewpoints, understanding, and positions.

To ensure that the interviews are successful, first decide on your area of interest (what you want to pursue in the interviews). Then schedule interviews with a few staff members (and clients, when permitted) who have specific knowledge of the particular area that is the most intriguing to you. You should be selective in your choice of interviewees, picking those who you think will best provide the information you need for your term paper and who are the most knowledgeable about your area of interest. Your agency supervisor can be helpful by directing you to willing and cooperative staff members and clients.

Preparing the Interview Guide

The next step is to prepare an interview guide. Serious thought should go into the production of your guide. The best way to begin is to think about things that may be puzzling to you. In quiet, reflective times during journal writing, ask yourself: "Am I feeling uncertain or confused about any aspect of the internship?" If so, begin to record relevant questions whenever these feelings of uncertainties occur. It is a good habit to have paper and pencil available at all times. I even keep a pad and pencil at my bedside for the occasions when I awake with a thought I may want to investigate in the morning. You will find that questions and thoughts arise at strange times, such as while your are riding in a bus, speaking with a friend, or watching television. Therefore, keeping a notebook handy can be advantageous.

Once you have refined your area of interest and sorted out what puzzles you, you are ready to draft a list of standard questions for the interviews. These standard questions will guarantee that each person you interview will be probed in a comparable manner. The sequence in which you conduct the interviews does not matter; what is important is that you cover every topic you have listed during the interview.

It is helpful for your interview guide to begin with a *face sheet* that covers the social characteristics of the interviewees. Although items for the face sheet vary, some of the most common are the person's name (or code number, if confidentiality is an issue), gender, age, education, race or ethnicity, residence (confidential in most law enforcement agencies), place and date of birth, and occupation, as well as the date and location of the interviews. Some of these items may be eliminated or additional items may be used, depending on the intentions of the interview. It is important to note that even though the face sheet is usually the first page, the questions on it are not always the initial ones that are asked. The topic, the level of trust that you and the interviewee have established, and other issues may influence whether you start at the face sheet or go directly into the interview. If you do the latter, you should eventually complete the face sheet for identification purposes.

During the interview, the emphasis should be on obtaining descriptions on or narratives of the person's feelings and thoughts. Therefore, it is preferable to compose open-ended questions. An example of an open-ended question is: "How do you feel about the working environment here?" This type of question allows the person to share his or her feelings on every aspect of the agency (if time permits). In contrast, a closed-end question such as "Is this a comfortable working environment for you?" may solicit a short and direct answer such as *yes* or *no*. If the person gives such an answer, you can follow up with a more direct question.

During the interview you should pay attention not only to what the person is saying, but to what he or she is not saying or is intimating through body language that you may consider significant. If this is your first experience with interviewing, I suggest that you first practice with friends and family members. The more you practice, the more comfortable you will feel during the actual interview.

Approaching Potential Interviewees

Once you have decided who you want to interview, contact each person individually to apprise him or her honestly and precisely of what you plan to cover in the interview and of how the interview will be conducted. All interviews should be conducted in the presence of your agency supervisor or assigned personel. As a courtesy you should explain the purpose of the interview and the criterion for the selection process.

Finally, tell the potential interviewees about your background and what stimulated your curiosity regarding the area of concern. It is easier to establish trust if you share something about yourself with them.

Two other important issues to address are confidentiality and tape recording. First, you should assure the interviewees that their names will not be used and that their answers will remain confidential. However, advise them that it is your duty to report any illegal behavior, so they should be cautious about admitting to this type of behavior. Second, if you plan to audiotape the interviews, ask the interviewees' permission beforehand and explain why you wish to do so.

Audio- and Videotaping Interviews

It is important to tape-record interviews because it is difficult to be attentive to everything an interviewee is saying if you are constantly writing. You must concentrate totally on the interview in a way that conveys that you are truly listening. However, do not fall into the trap of not listening to the interviewee because you think you will be able to catch everything later while listening to the tape. For example, tapes can be garbled, the interviewee may perceive that you are not truly interested, or you may miss subtle nuances of expression. Occasional note taking, such as writing key words or phrases, is a good method of combating this tendency.

If a person does not want to be audiotaped, you will have to rely on your note-taking and recall skills. Note taking is a process of keeping in touch with what is going on in an interview. As Lofland and Lofland (1984, p. 61) noted: "You take notes on what has already gone on, and notes on what should go on—what has now come up that you should ask about before the interview is over." Make sure that you write up your notes or transcripts of audiotaped interviews immediately after the interviews while the information is fresh in your mind to ensure that you are recording the most recent views and ideas.

In some agencies you will be given access to clients' files. While you are privy to this personal information, the issue of *confidentiality* should be constantly in your thoughts. It is important to learn with whom you are at liberty to discuss the contents of the files in the agency. The background information contained in the files may be invaluable in assisting you to develop an outline for your area of interest.

SELECTING, DESIGNATING, AND CHANGING AN INTERNSHIP

Internship coordinators have many factors to consider when matching students with agency supervisors. The first factor should be a student's preference. Sometimes, however, it may not be possible to do so, as when there are more requests for a placement than the agency supervisor can adequately supervise. For example, in my program, the Secret Service will only take two interns per semester from each neighboring college and university. This placement is so popular that I have to reserve placements a year in advance. Thus, if students want to work at this agency, they must apply in their junior year to be considered for placement in their senior year. The Secret Service also requires a lengthy background check that takes two to three months.

The second factor is a student's skill-development needs. It is important for your internship coordinator to match your skill level with the appropriate agency supervisor. For instance, if you need a structured environment to assist you in developing organizational skills, it will be helpful for you to be assigned to a supervisor who has time for a daily, one-on-one relationship. If you happen to have low self-confidence, you should be placed with a supervisor who can be patient and supportive of you. Although it is not always possible to make a perfect match, your internship coordinator can provide the best possible match based on both your and the agency supervisor's personality characteristics because of his or her relationship over time with various agency supervisors.

It is essential for you and your internship coordinator to establish a communication pattern, either by in-person meetings or telephone conferences. For small internship classes (less than 20 students), biweekly telephone conferences are recommended. I have found that within two weeks, my interns and the agency supervisors know whether there has been a positive match. If not, there is still ample time to relocate the intern with enough hours left to have a meaningful experience with a new agency.

As internship supervisor, I request a midterm evaluation from the agency supervisor, which requires a mid-internship meeting between the student and agency supervisor, during which the student's experience and performance up to that time are assessed and goals are set for the remaining time. During this meeting, it is also appropriate for you to address any concerns or problems that you have been experiencing with your agency supervisor and internship coordinator. In addition, it is important for you to tell your internship coordinator about any problems you are having with the agency supervisor in case these problems result in a negative evaluation. The internship coordinator needs this information to evaluate whether this is a favorable placement for professional and personal development and to determine if the site should be used in the future. See Chapter 9 for further discussion.

Whereas most internship placements are positive, you may not have a good relationship with your agency supervisor for various reasons, such as personnel problems, unforeseen crises, or other personal issues. If you encounter inadequate supervision for any reason, get in touch with your internship coordinator immediately for assistance in either transferring supervision within the agency or, if it is early enough in the semester, to find a new agency and supervisor.

PEER SUPPORT

In addition to the major roles played by your internship coordinator and agency supervisor in the success of your internship experience, your peers who are taking the same internship course or who have taken it previously may provide tremendous support. For example, they may be able to recommend potential sites or warn you against others (bearing in mind that you should consider this information carefully—people can view the same experience differently). If one of your peers confides that the placement only offered clerical work with little staff and no client contact, you may want to question the limitations of the learning opportunity provided by that agency.

Peers who share the same placement can also provide a feeling of comradeship. Although your internship coordinator and agency supervisor may try to relate to you and give you support, your peers are likely to share the same feelings of being over-whelmed, anxious, and incompetent and to listen to your feelings and concerns. Once you establish a bond with them, your feeling of being alone is usually diminished, you can learn how they are coping, and it becomes easier to work through this period.

Some criminal justice agencies function differently from others, depending on their locations. For instance, a police department in a rural area functions differently from one in an urban or suburban area. The differences among these locations may be apparent in their managerial styles, communication techniques, and agency interactions. If any of your peers have completed internship courses in these different settings, they can give you significant information that can help you decide where you want to work.

It may not always be possible for you and your peers to have a reciprocal sup-porting relationship. Therefore, it is important for you to realize and accept that there will be times when you may be able to help each other. When circumstances dictate, advise your peer to consult with the agency supervisor or internship coordinator, and you do the same.

Peer support may be provided in ways other than dealing with crises. You may schedule periodic meetings during agency break times or plan outside activities to provide support on a regular basis. Also, your internship coordinator may do as I do and schedule three seminars a semester that allow time for peer discussions and support.

CASE STUDY: ONE STUDENT'S PERSPECTIVE

The following is a perspective on "Internship Heaven" and "Internship Nightmares" by Jason Khoury, who completed an internship in April 1993. Although Jason worked in a criminal justice agency, he developed relationships with students in other fields and felt a need to include their views in his discussion of a wide range of internships in his term paper.

Internship Heaven

In some ways, it seems like an internship is all glory for a student (receiving an intern-ship with the Secret Service was certainly a high point in my life). According to Chastain (1992, p. 172), internships are "hunting licenses" for students in that they give students an opportunity to "hunt for useful experiences" in corporations or the govern-ment. Picture a college sociology major, one of tens of thousands, if not hundreds of thousands, in the country, who is nearing graduation in an economy that looks bleak. In his last semester, the student obtains an internship with the Office of the State Attorney, which hires him after he graduates. This scenario may seem like a dream, but it's a reality. A number of corporations, including Allstate Insurance and Aetna Life, have extensive internship programs through which they screen potential employees and hire many of them (Scott, 1992).

Students may also become known throughout particular industries through articles in trade journals. For example, the American Physical Society (APS) has been placing interns since 1978 and getting them known and hired. The experiences of interns who are chosen by APS are often written up in such journals such as Physics Today. Articles on them include where they have interned and what they have done (see for example, "Industrial Internships," 1991). Students who are mentioned in these articles not only can add this information to their résumé, but become known throughout their field.

Most local district and state attorneys offices offer internships, as do local police departments and federal law enforcement agencies. And public and private schools have long drawn on student teachers to help out in the classroom. Even the U.S. Congress gets into the act. In the years following John F. Kennedy's famous call to public service, congressmen got together and formed internship programs to give students experience in working for the federal government, which had been regarded as a poor career choice after the escalation of the war in Vietnam and the antigovernment student movement. In 1973, Congress created the LBJ Internship Program to allow every House office to pay students for summer internships, so youths who couldn't afford to come to Washington and intern could do so (Greenberg, 1990).

Internship Nightmares

Although many companies value their internship programs, some of their employees do not. Many student interns report bosses who "simply don't want them there. The managers are unable or unwilling to teach, coach, or develop the interns" (Scott, 1992, p. 62). In other words, the interns are treated with an utter lack of professionalism by the people who could one day be their fellow workers. For interns who are stuck with people who do not want them there, a semester or summer could truly be a hellish mix of put-downs and meaningless tasks.

Considering Jason's descriptions, I would assume that the students who were hired by the Office of the State Attorney, the Juvenile Court, the Metropolitan Correctional Center of Miami, and the Coral Gables Police Department experienced *internship heaven.*

I can recall a placement, however, where a student was an *internship nightmare.* For the purpose of confidentiality we will call the student Ms. B.

After one week at her placement Ms. B. came to me and explained that she was extremely uncomfortable in the juvenile detention center. After a lengthy discussion, I agreed to place her in the juvenile alternative sanctions system (a less threatening environment). Two weeks later her supervisor called to inform me of a confrontation between them, wherein Ms. B. used profanity, and made the decision to terminate her placement. I contacted Ms. B. and was informed (with the use of profanity) that "they just don't like me and they don't want me there." After a brief period Ms. B. became calm and agreed to return and apologize to her supervisor. I called her supervisor and informed her that Ms. B. would be returning and apologizing. The next day I received a fax stating the following:

Dr. Taylor:

As agreed, we are faxing you documentation and evaluation of Ms. B. Ms. B. did not call yesterday as specifically instructed to do so by you. Therefore, we have no choice but to terminate her. This morning at 8:40 A.M. Ms. Nichols had a call/message from her. Ms. B. stated that everything was OK and she would not be in today because she has a doctor's appointment, but she would be in tomorrow. As of now, we still consider Ms. B. terminated and will *consider* reinstating her if she does *all* of the following:

1. Apologizes to all parties concerned.
2. Meets with supervisory staff to discuss her overall unsatisfactory job performance.
3. Adheres to guidelines, directives, and corrective action plan developed by supervisory staff.

We will keep you abreast of new developments as they arise.

The short version of the conclusion is that Ms. B. returned to the agency for one week and, according to the supervisor, she "became arrogant, defensive, confrontive, disrespectful, and rude and left. She did not complete her 240 hours. She could not be contacted by telephone and did not return to my office."

The following is an incident report that was submitted to an agency supervisor regarding an internship nightmare experienced by one of our students (Ms. G).

Subject: Incident Involving Lt. C and Det. M

I request that you look into the situation reported below, since it could affect my status as an intern and/or my future in a law enforcement career.

On June 26, 1997, at approximately 8:00 P.M., while riding with the Street Narcotics Unit (SNU), an unrelated incident took place in the area in which the SNU was operating. I remained with Officer M while other officers from the SNU proceeded to the area of the second incident. I learned eventually that the second incident had to do with a police shooting.

In the early morning hours of June 27, 1997, I received a call from Sergeant N of the Homicide Unit. I was told to come immediately to the central station to have my statement taken regarding what I had witnessed. I proceeded to the station, where I arrived at 6:00 A.M. I was held there until 10:30 A.M., even after I had stated several times that I had to go to work. I was questioned by Lt. C, Sgt. N, and Det. M regarding the incident and I replied truthfully and to the best of my knowledge to their questions. They insituated that I was covering something up and that I was not being totally honest in my answers, even to the extent that they submitted me to a voice stress analyzer. As a result of the test, Det. M told me I was being deceptive. I informed him I was telling them what I best recollected from the previous evening.

On July 2, 1997 I was called by Lt. C, who asked me to come to the station once again. I was questioned about my previous answers. I was told by Lt. C and Det. M that I had not been truthful. Lt. C told me that he did not want to see me "get myself in trouble for hiding something"; he also stated that I was "jeopardizing my career in this field and my life." Due to what I perceived as threats and Det. M's yelling at me, I claimed that I was not a criminal and should not be treated as such. Det. M indicated that "the jails are full of innocent people." I responded to both Lt. C and Det. M that I had been truthful in my previous responses, and that I should not be treated as a common criminal. The detective indicated that I was there on the scene as an observer and that my job was to observe, and "I had not observed s---."

I feel that I have been treated unfairly in this matter. I have cooperated fully and truthfully, yet I am viewed differently by those conducting the inquiry in the above-mentioned matter. I have spoken to my internship coordinator at the university and have been advised to discontinue my riding assignments until she speaks with you and clarifies the situation.

The student was not required to return to this field placement, but did complete her hours at another site. She was, however, summoned to appear at the trial of the accused officer, but was not called to testify. She may be ordered to appear at an upcoming trial for another officer allegedly involved in the incident. After which, hopefully, her nightmare will be over.

SUMMARY

In your internship, you may think that you are filling two roles: as a student and as an employee. It is important for you to remember, however, that you are primarily a student in the role of a participant observer and secondarily, an employee, and as a participant-observer your objectives are to absorb all you can about your agency as it applies to your desired goal of entering the field of criminal justice–criminology and recording staff interactions and agency events and situations objectively.

Once you determine what is important for you to observe, you need to decide the method you want to use to record your observations. In this chapter it is recommended that you keep a journal for recording your daily experiences. Some supervisors suggest the use of a diary (similar to a journal), which is set up like a calendar but includes no systematic way of recording data, whereas others suggest the use of logbooks or field notebooks. Whatever method you use, you must remember to maintain confidentiality whenever you write or discuss your entries.

The most popular interviewing method is the personal interview, which may be conducted with or without a tape recorder. If you choose to audiotape the interviews, it is necessary to get permission from the interviewees before you do so. Prior to the interviews, you should also have a good notion of the areas or subjects on which you will focus in collecting and recording the desired information.

Preparing an interview guide can contribute to successful interviews with a few staff members who have specific knowledge of your area of interest. For the purpose of organization, the guide should include a face sheet that covers the social characteristics of the interviewees. When confidentiality is an issue, use a code number instead of a name on the face sheet.

As an intern, the most important thing to remember is to do your best. This does not necessarily mean that you must be everything to everybody. It is important to set high standards for yourself but to understand the difference between high standards and unreasonable expectations. Above all, keep in mind that your primary goal is to learn, not to demonstrate what you know. You should expect the agency staff to be more educated and experienced than you, but you should not allow their training to intimidate you. Their expertise is what you are counting on to provide you with one of the most exciting educational experiences of your life. Relax, go for it, and take advantage of this great opportunity.

Agency Supervision

Questions for Students

Who will provide supervision
during your internship?

What type of relationship will
you have with your
supervisor?

Why do you need to
understand the supervisory
process?

THE AGENCY'S PERSPECTIVE

From the agency's perspective, internship programs provide them with a valuable pool of job applicants. Since most internships in the criminal justice system do not pay stipends, some interns have stated that they consider internships a source of cheap labor (Khoury, 1993). Although some agencies use interns to perform menial tasks, such as running errands or performing secretarial tasks, including filing, photocopying, and typing, most agencies consider internship programs a tremendous benefit to them. As one agency executive put it: "There are reams of hard and soft benefits that make intern programs an invaluable recruitment tool" (quoted in Scott, 1992, p. 60).

Several of my students have been hired by the Office of the State Attorney, the Department of Corrections, and various other criminal justice agencies after they completed their internships. Their agency supervisors have told me that interns who are reliable, hardworking, and personable and who demonstrate the skills necessary to perform the tasks required for available positions are the first to be considered for job openings because their agency supervisors have firsthand knowledge of their character and ability. In any case, interns will become recruiters for these agencies by encouraging other students on campus to apply for these internship placements. This process fits with the goals of agencies whose primary way of filling entry-level positions is by recruiting recent college graduates (Scott, 1992, p. 62).

Internship programs are also cost-effective because agencies do not have to allocate funds for campus-recruitment programs if their interns are doing the recruiting. According to Chastain (1992, p. 180), a good program uses the interns' time to "produce as useful an output as possible [and] that causes the intern to want to seek post-graduation employment in the company."

DEFINING FIELD SUPERVISION

The first considerations for many students in choosing an internship placement are the clients (adults or juveniles), location of the agency and concerns about transportation, and hours of operation (whether the agency is open in the evenings and on weekends). Although these are important concerns, it has been my experience that supervision by and interaction with the professionals with whom you will work is the most important factor to be considered.

During your internship experience, you will be under the supervision of a faculty member from your college or university (the internship coordinator) and a staff member at the placement site (the agency supervisor). As discussed at greater length in Chapter 9, the internship coordinator observes your progress and interfaces with your agency supervisor and other appropriate staff members at the internship site.

In your fieldwork you will work closely with your agency supervisor while reporting regularly to your internship coordinator. They are both responsible for monitoring the performance of your daily assignments and should be kept completely informed of your activities and notified immediately of any difficulties or problems you may have that would impede your individual and professional growth.

Therefore, the basic question you must ask yourself about a supervisor is whether you can work with this person and if he or she is interested in helping you learn. For many internship placements, the internship coordinators have made previous site visits and are acquainted with the agency supervisors and their qualifications. For those of you who must find your own placements, it is important to consider the supervisor's personality, qualifications, areas of interest, and desire and ability to provide adequate time for supervision and training. It is also important to know whether you need a more nurturing environment in which the supervisor provides a great deal of direction (the agency-centered model of supervision) or less direction and greater autonomy (the student-centered model of supervision). In summary, you should select a supervisor with the ability and willingness to work with you to meet best your personal and educational needs.

Most agencies use a student-centered model of supervision, whereby students must arrange their interactions with the internship coordinator, the agency supervisor, and their peers and determine the amount of supervisory interaction they want to have (Gordon and McBride, 1990, p. 48). The agency-centered model of supervision that is being used more and more frequently (see Figure 8.1). In this model, interns' interactions are coordinated by the chief executive officers (president and vice president) of the organization.

It is not unusual for students initially to feel dependent on their supervisors. For example, one of my students reported that her first day in a prison internship was strange. Her supervisor had to attend a meeting and left her with other staff members who "did not know what to do" with her. During the course of your internship, your relationship with your supervisor will become less dependent and more reciprocal with an exchange of the supervisor's feedback and your input.

ROLE OF THE AGENCY SUPERVISOR

The agency supervisor plays a crucial role in guiding a student's training experiences and in most cases will long be remembered as a key motivator. Located at the site, the supervisor can provide educational opportunities that are impossible to obtain in the classroom. In a successful placement, the supervisor will become a supportive and skilled mentor whom you will view as a role model for your future professional life. Unfortunately, this has not been the case for some interns who have found the relationship with their supervisors to be inadequate and demeaning. In such a case, your only recourse is to report any incidents to your internship coordinator, since the

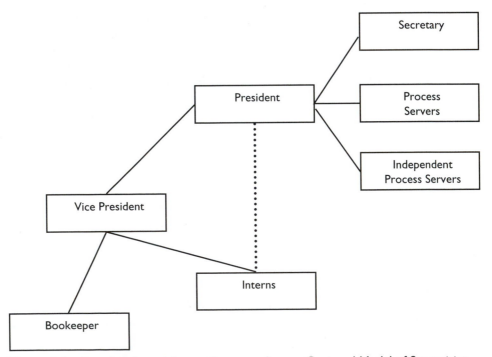

Figure 8.1   Sample Informal Agency Structure: Agency-Centered Model of Supervision—Organizational Breakdown

evaluation of supervisors is often a sensitive issue in an agency and rarely covers work with interns (Norcross et al., 1988).

The best ways to get to know potential supervisors is to have personal meetings or phone interview with them. It is my practice to have interns phone and schedule personal interviews. Along with other pertinent information, such as your academic training and practical experiences, mentioned in Chapter 3, the supervisor will be interested in your personality, reliability, work ethic, and how well you follow instructions. These factors will assist the supervisor in assessing if it will be worth the time to supervise you.

Once you and your internship coordinator know that a particular supervisor can devote sufficient time to your learning experience, you should make arrangements to sign an internship agreement that specifies the terms of the internship and type of work you will perform. See Figure 8.2 for a sample of the internship agreement used

---

Name of Intern_____

Dear Intern Supervisor:

To provide our interns with the best possible learning experience, we ask that you consider the following agreement between the Department of Sociology Internship Office and your agency.

The agency agrees to:

...provide meaningful criminal justice related activity to the student. Clerical work, filing, phone answering, etc. will be kept at a minimum;

...contact the Internship Coordinator if any questions or problems arise with the student or the program itself;

...the best of its ability, not to put the student in a life-threatening situation;

...not use the student in an undercover capacity;

...monitor the student's hours and make sure he/she puts in the required 240 hours during the semester;

...evaluate each intern twice during the semester.

The Intern Supervisor will be responsible for addressing safety issues, policy and procedures and other relevant information, with each intern.

The Intern Supervisor agrees that the Internship Coordinator may visit during the semester to meet with the supervisor and the student.

We look forward to an exciting year for our interns and thank you for your participation in our program.

_____ Date	_____ Date
Department of Sociology Internship Coordinator	Internship Supervisor
	_____
	Position
	_____
	Agency

Figure 8.2   Sample Internship Agency Agreement

in my course. Along with this agreement, you should be given information on your routine, hours, the agency's rules and regulations, and schedule for supervision.

Your agency supervisor should inform you of the appropriate codes of dress and conduct as well. He or she should determine the availability and appropriateness of supplemental reading material and make a general timetable for orientation and ongoing fieldwork activities. It is desirable for your agency supervisor to provide purposeful contact with the realities of the agency's day-to-day work. He or she should make sure that your work assignments throughout the term depend on your learning needs and abilities, keeping in mind that your work should be of value to the agency but that you should not have the same workload as a regular employee. Because it is not always possible to work with your agency supervisor on a daily basis, you and your supervisor should arrange regular sessions to discuss weekly events, goals that have been accomplished, future goals, and the status of your professional development. In short, your relationship with the agency supervisor serves as the medium through which you can make maximum use of the knowledge you bring to the placement and can be helped to develop your skills and accept new concepts and ideas.

SUMMARY

During your internship experience, you will be under the supervision of your internship coordinator and agency supervisor. Although the agency supervisor is responsible for the quality of your work, his or her major concern should be with accomplishing the primary task of learning. The basic question is whether you can work with your supervisor and whether the supervisor is interested in helping you learn.

The relationship between you and your agency supervisor serves as the medium through which you are able to make maximum use of the knowledge you bring to the placement and are helped to develop your skills and accept new concepts and ideas. Your agency supervisor should encourage you to discuss your feelings and attitudes about your work experiences and help you resolve work-related problems. He or she should also evaluate your progress—or lack thereof—*with you*. You should receive credit for what you are doing well and comments on needed areas of improvement.

It is not unusual for interns initially to feel a sense of dependence on their supervisors. During the course of your internship, your relationship with your supervisor will become less dependent and more reciprocal, with an exchange of the supervisor's feedback and your input. The introduction to your peer support system will also contribute to a diminished feeling of dependence. Your peers will give you tremendous support by providing a sense of comradeship and valuable information on potential internship sites. Your first consideration may be the client population you will serve during your internship. Despite the importance of this concern, the most significant factor in your development will be your ability to perceive the value of the supervisory process and to use it frequently.

c h a p t e r   9

Faculty Supervision

Questions for Students

What do you think is the role of your faculty supervisor?

What are your previous encounters with faculty supervision?

Do you think that supervision is important to personal and professional development?

ROLE OF THE FACULTY SUPERVISOR

Interns are supervised by a faculty supervisor and an agency supervisor. This chapter focuses on the faculty supervisor. This type of supervision differs from agency supervision, in which there is constant monitoring of your performance. The amount of faculty supervision you receive will depend largely on you and your need to pursue it in meeting your goal of enhancing your personal and professional development. This should be a mutual relationship, with you giving input and the faculty supervisor providing constructive feedback, and the relationship should move from dependence to interdependence to independence. This relationship will move through these steps more easily if both of you are able to express your fears. My students have shared their fears of not being able to perform required tasks well enough to receive satisfactory evaluations and of appearing "stupid," and I have shared my fears with them of interns doing something that will jeopardize themselves or the agency placement for future interns. Because faculty supervisors are ultimately accountable for ensuring that interns meet professional and educational standards, they are extremely concerned about the interns' attitudes toward performing high-quality work at the agencies, as well as the interns' academic performance. Therefore, the primary responsibility of faculty supervisors is to ensure that all interns are prepared and apply themselves diligently and responsibly to fulfill their obligations to the agencies and the university.

Although the university and the agency accept shared accountability for designing useful assignments and other educational events to fulfill the instructional goals of the internship program, the faculty supervisor shoulders the primary responsibility for administering and managing field education and acts as a liaison between the school and the agency. The faculty supervisor will determine the course requirements and direct your internship education and enter into an agreement with your agency supervisor that you will be given the opportunity to observe and participate in various agency assignments.

ADMINISTRATIVE AND MANAGEMENT RESPONSIBILITIES

The internship coordinator provides leadership in

1. Developing and monitoring placements
2. Placing and replacing students
3. Devising methods of obtaining necessary information for making placements
4. Determining the criteria for the internship course
5. Developing and implementing policies and procedures related to fieldwork
6. Designating field (agency) supervisors
7. Representing the university in relationships with agencies

To determine the most suitable field placement for a student, the faculty supervisor meets with the student to discuss the student's concerns and professional aspirations. At this time, the faculty supervisor asks the student to fill out various forms to provide additional information necessary for establishing a proper field placement and gives the student a copy of the syllabus. (See Figure 9.1 for a sample syllabus)

After the student is placed in an agency, the faculty supervisor monitors the student's performance, and if deemed unsuitable (a rare occurrence), the faculty supervisor arranges for the student to be placed in a more appropriate agency; this decision should be made early enough in the process so that the student has the opportunity to fulfill the requirements of the second placement.

If a student finds his or her own placement (for example, one that is closer to home during the summer when he or she is not taking other classes on campus), the faculty supervisor first determines that the student's work will be of value to the particular agency. Then he or she contacts the agency the student has suggested, establishes a relationship with the agency supervisor, and makes sure that the agency will provide the appropriate experience for the student. (For the role of the agency supervisor, see Chapter 8.)

Term Paper:_____

DUE DATE:

INTERNSHIP GRADE

The following will determine your final grade:

1. agency supervisor's (midterm) evaluation
2. agency supervisor's (final) evaluation
3. internship (term) paper

TEXTBOOK

Taylor, Dorothy L., *Jumpstarting Your Career: An Internship Guide for Criminal Justice*, Prentice Hall, 1998. It is suggested that you read the entire text. However, Chapters 1 through 4 and 6 are required. Chapters 1 through 3 should be read before you begin your internship; they will be helpful in establishing your goals and objectives for this course. Chapters 4 and 6 will be useful for the term paper.

SUPERVISOR EVALUATIONS

The agency supervisor will evaluate your performance twice during the semester. The first evaluation serves primarily to indicate any problem areas (see the sample evaluation form).

The faculty supervisor will discuss these evaluations with you. **IT IS YOUR RESPONSIBILITY TO MAKE SURE THESE EVALUATIONS ARE COMPLETED AND SUBMITTED.**

INTERNSHIP TERM PAPER

You will submit a *detailed* outline before you to submit the final paper.

Present the term paper in an observation/participation style. Compare what you observed and experienced in the "real world" or at your agency with the criminological concepts and issues you learned in the classroom (see the sample outline in Figure 9.2).

The term paper should be typed double spaced. It should also be free of spelling and grammatical errors and should include a bibliography, with all sources properly cited. The paper should be at least 15 pages.

Figure 9.1   Sample Syllabus

ADVISEMENT AND LIAISON ACTIVITIES

Along with academic advisement, the faculty supervisor provides support to the student when emotional or interpersonal difficulties occur during the field placement. As was stated earlier, it is helpful for faculty supervisors and interns to relate honestly at the beginning of their relationship about their shared and individual needs and concerns. This will eliminate much anxiety, ineffective communication, and frustration. Baird's (1996, p. 58) list of supervisors' and interns' needs to be considered is helpful:

- *Supervisors' needs:* honesty and integrity, ethical conduct, openness to suggestion, respect for the supervisor's experience, careful work of high quality, deep thought, hard work, and willingness to listen even if there is disagreement
- *Interns' needs:* support, patience, knowledge of the field, guidance, accessibility, modeling, direct teaching of information, involvement, some autonomy, trust, openness, and willingness to listen.

To prevent interns from making mistakes and to help them achieve the most beneficial learning experience, it is crucial for the faculty supervisor to explain his or her requirements to interns at the onset of their internships. The interns should know the frequency and time of supervisory meetings, the content of the meetings (for example, for group discussions or individual journal reviews), and whether both personal and professional issues will be dealt with.

The faculty supervisor makes a minimum of three site visits per academic semester: (1) before the student is placed (in some cases during the preceding semester), (2) during the week of midterm examinations, and (3) before the week of final examinations. Additional visits are made, when necessary, to support the student's instructional agenda. The faculty supervisor also maintains regular telephone contact with the student (as well as with first-time agency supervisors), especially during the initial phase of placement, to resolve problems immediately. Although inappropriate placements are rare, early visits and telephone calls by your faculty supervisor to the agency can determine that you have been inappropriately placed to obtain the desired internship experience. For example, one site visit and two follow-up telephone calls determined that one of our interns, who was placed in a residential treatment program for delinquent adolescent girls expecting to have one-on-one contact by tutoring the girls, was working on the switchboard most of the time. This student was reassigned to another agency, where she experienced a more fulfilling internship.

ACADEMIC ASSIGNMENTS

Your faculty supervisor will influence your internship education significantly through assigned readings, journal reports, observations of various features of the agency environment, and term papers. Your journal reports and other written communications will assist your faculty supervisor in overseeing your progress and enable him or her to help you solve any problems or strengthen any weaknesses that may be interfering with your personal and professional growth. It is natural to want to avoid discussing your weakness or concerns for fear of receiving an unsatisfactory grade, but if you are not meeting the agency's requirements, you will almost guarantee an unsatisfactory grade. Your faculty supervisor anticipates that some problems may occur, and that you may experience some anxieties regarding your performance during your introductory experience with criminal justice professionals.

During the internship experience, students assume the role of participant-observers. They investigate the setting, the role of the various staff members, individuals, and the activity of the agency. In periodic seminars (at least three per semester), they present ongoing situations from their current work in their field agencies to their faculty supervisor and fellow internship students, and during finals week, they submit a direct-observation term paper of their internship experience. (For a sample outline for a term paper, see Figure 9.2.)

EVALUATION AND GRADING

The faculty supervisor is responsible for assigning the final letter grade in fieldwork, in consultation with the agency supervisor, at the end of the semester in which the student

I. INTRODUCTION
   A. *Brief* overview of the agency, including:
      1. Type of agency (local, state, federal, law enforcement, court, corrections, and so forth)
      2. Size
      3. History
   B. Organizational structure (including your location in that structure)
      1. Goals
      2. Objectives

II. REVIEW OF THE CRIMINOLOGY LITERATURE
   A. A discussion of issues, problems, and practices relevant to the agency (such as budget constraints, legal changes, increasing crime rates, effects of prison over-crowding, effects of increasing public attitudes toward getting tough on crime)
   B. How does the literature address these issues?
   C. Refer to both published articles and books and course work materials (textbook or class notes)

III. PLACEMENT AGENCY: OBSERVATIONS AND FINDINGS
   A. What actually happens in the agency?
      1. What do you do?
      2. According to the agency, what issues, problems, and practices are most important?
   B. Review selected agency documents
      1. Describe any differences you have observed in the formal and informal structure of the agency (see Chapter 4 of the textbook).

IV. SUMMARY AND DISCUSSION
   A. Synthesize your agency placement experience and themes from the criminology literature and course materials.
   B. How has your criminological understanding been enhanced or changed by this experience?
      1. What ideas have helped you understand your experience?
      2. What works? What does not?

V. BIBLIOGRAPHY: See any criminal justice/criminology textbook for the proper format.

Figure 9.2   Sample Outline for Term Paper

interned. It should be noted, however, that the evaluation of students is an ongoing process and that each seminar is considered a period of evaluation. The faculty super-visor is at a disadvantage in that he or she cannot directly observe the interns' perfor-mance at the fieldwork sites. Other than sporadic visits to the agencies and occasion-al telephone conferences with the agency supervisors, the faculty supervisor must rely on the agency supervisors' views of students' accomplishments in the field. Therefore, the faculty supervisor grades students on the basis of the agency supervisors' two field evaluations (see Figure 9.3 for a sample evaluation form) and the students' achieve-ment of goals, participation in seminar, field notes, and term papers. The weight of each of these elements in determining the students' final grades differs, depending on the grading system used by a particular faculty supervisor.

Student's Name   _____
Social Security No.   _____
Agency   _____
Intern's Agency
Supervisor   _____
Position   _____
Address of Agency   _____
Phone No. of Agency   _____

YOUR COOPERATION IN MAKING THIS INTERNSHIP AVAILABLE TO OUR STU-
DENTS IS GREATLY APPRECIATED. AS THE INTERNSHIP DRAWS TO A CLOSE, IT
WOULD BE MOST HELPFUL TO ME IF YOU WOULD COMPLETE THIS EVALUA-
TION FORM AND RETURN YOUR COMMENTS TO ME IN THE SELF-ADDRESSED
ENVELOPE THAT IS ENCLOSED.

THIS EVALUATION IS AN EXTREMELY IMPORTANT TOOL IN PROVIDING INFOR-
MATION PARAMOUNT TO THE STUDENT'S ACADEMIC AND PROFESSIONAL
DEVELOPMENT. I WILL REVIEW THE EVALUATION WITH THE STUDENT. A COPY
OF THE EVALUATION WILL BE PLACED IN THE STUDENT'S FILE.

IF YOU THINK THAT FURTHER COMMENTS ARE NECESSARY, FEEL FREE TO PRO-
VIDE ADDITIONAL INFORMATION OR ENCLOSURES.

THANK YOU FOR YOUR INVALUABLE ASSISTANCE IN THIS INTERNSHIP PRO-
GRAM AND YOUR CONTRIBUTION TO OUR STUDENTS' EDUCATION.

1. Identify the general and specific roles and duties (observational, participatory, counseling,
   and so forth) assumed by the student, the overall responsibilities entrusted to the student,
   and the learning objectives established for the student.

2. Evaluate the student's ability to satisfy the objectives set forth for student interns by
   your agency.

Figure 9.3   Sample Student Internship Evaluation

3. Briefly describe the specific areas in which the student demonstrated particular abilities favorable to your profession.

4. In which areas would you suggest that the student concentrate his or her efforts to improve in order to achieve future success in the profession?

5. How would you rate the student's overall performance? Please circle one of the descriptions below:

Excellent   Above average   Average   Below average   Poor

6. Did you discuss this evaluation with the student?

Yes_____   No_____

Figure 9.3   Sample Student Internship Evaluation *(cont'd)*

ADVOCACY AND GRIEVANCE PROCEDURES

If you have a grievance with your agency supervisor, discuss it with the supervisor. However, there are exceptions. You may encounter some problems that should be discussed with your faculty supervisor before you confront your agency supervisor. These problems may be ethical (accepting free food while on ride-alongs with police officers) or methodological (observing a difference from theory to practice, such as violations of *Miranda* rights). If you and your agency supervisor cannot resolve your difficulties, you should confer with the faculty supervisor or with another faculty member, the department chairperson, or the dean. When there is a controversy regarding grades, you should comply with the university's policy on reassessing grades.

SUMMARY

During the internship, the student will be afforded one primary (faculty) and two secondary (agency and peer) sources of supervision. This chapter has focused on the role
of the faculty supervisor. (See Chapter 8 for the role of the agency and peer supervisors.) Supervision is the fundamental instructional goal necessary for the student to
develop personally and professionally. The skills learned by achieving this goal will
prove beneficial throughout the student's professional career. The student will largely
determine the amount of supervision that he or she needs to strengthen his or her personal and professional development. Although this should be a mutual relationship
between the student and the faculty supervisor, the faculty supervisor is ultimately
responsible for the student's preparedness and ability to carry out his or her obligations to the agency and the university. One key to positive career development is the
ability to acknowledge the need for supervision and to acquire support when necessary. Another key is the ability to communicate effectively with the faculty supervisor
by being honest and ethical. Finally, students should be familiar with grievance procedures, and if controversy regarding evaluations by the faculty supervisor or grades
from the internship coordinator arises, comply with the university's grievance policies.

c h a p t e r   1 0

Values and Ethical Standards

Questions for Students

How does your value system affect your attitude and and behavior toward your clients?

Why do ethical guidelines exist?

What common ethical and moral dilemmas may you be faced with during your internship?

THE INTERN'S VALUE SYSTEM

What are your values, social principles, and standards? Your values will play an important role in how you adhere to the ethical standards set forth in the criminal justice system. Not only is it necessary for you to understand your own values, it is important for you to be openminded about the values of the agency's staff and clients. If you have negative feelings toward people who are involved in the criminal justice system, this may not be the place for you to intern or the profession for you to consider. You may dislike these people's lifestyles and values, but your feelings should not influence your professionalism.

During this internship, another part of your experience will be finding out more about yourself and evaluating or reevaluating your own values. For instance, you may consider yourself to be a broadminded person and be amazed to discover that you are experiencing feelings of prejudice and a reluctance to treat some clients impartially. Granted, this may be a painful lesson, but it may also be the most important lesson

93

you learn during your internship, so you will "do no harm"—the first ethical rule of interning (Bairn, 1996, p. 28). Once you recover from this bombshell, you may become more accepting of people with different values; if you cannot, you will not be effective with others. It is not unusual to have this experience, and sharing your feelings with your supervisors, other staff members, and peers can help you survive this trying time.

While interning in the criminal justice system, you may work with staff members who have become burned out and may try to influence you to adopt their skeptical and harsh attitudes toward clients. Because you will want to establish a good relationship with these staff members, you may find yourself in a situation that may compromise your values. When such a situation occurs, it is important not to let anyone influence your thinking. You will be more effective if you make your own assessments of others, and you will also ensure that you provide high-quality treatment and exhibit good ethical principles.

ETHICAL PRINCIPLES FOR CRIMINAL JUSTICE PROFESSIONALS

Criminal justice is a multidisciplinary profession, consisting of judges, lawyers, psychiatrists, psychologists, social workers, and other helping professionals. As an intern you may be working with an agency supervisor from any of these disciplines. To guarantee high-quality treatment and lessen the possibility of harm to clients, many professions have instituted formal ethical codes and principles. The states also attempt to shield clients by establishing laws to oversee the licensing and practice of many professions. Violations of these ethical codes and laws may result in the loss of the right to practice; for instance, a judge may be impeached and removed from the bench, or a psychiatrist may lose his or her license.

All professions do not have identical codes of ethics, but their codes share certain basic principles (Kitchener, 1984). The following are some of the codes under which many agency supervisors may be working:

- American Bar Association Code of Ethics
- American Counseling Association Code of Ethics and Standards of Practice
- Code of Ethical Principles for Marriage and Family Therapists
- Ethical Principles and Code of Conduct of psychologists
- Ethical Standards for School Counselors
- NASW (National Association of Social Workers) Code of Ethics

The lack of a formal code of ethics or standards for the criminal justice system has become a matter of concern in teaching ethics in criminal justice. To address this issue, Kleinig and Smith (1997) edited a collection of invitational essays, originally presented at a workshop at John Jay College of Criminal Justice, on teaching criminal justice ethics. The authors of these essays, who are experts in practical and professional ethics, applied the knowledge they had gained from teaching in other areas, such as law, psychology, education, medicine, and social work, to criminal justice ethics. The questions they raised included the following: What should instructors be trying to achieve in teaching criminal justice ethics? How best may they go about it? How can they tell if they have succeeded? It is hoped that the essays related to these questions will increase the resources available to instructors in integrating an ethics component into the criminal justice curriculum. Having been a social worker before I became a criminologist, I tend to use the NASW Code of Ethics. Some ethical issues that I have found most relevant for interns in my program are confidentiality, competence, corruption, and dual relationships. (See Figure 10.1 for a sample ethical agreement form.)

As an intern, you are expected to follow certain ethical guidelines for your benefit and protection, as well as for those of clients, internship supervisors and agencies, and the internship coordinator and university. Whenever you have questions about ethical conduct, you should discuss them with your agency supervisor or internship coordinator. The following are the minimum ethical standards that you, as an intern, must agree to follow:

CONFIDENTIALITY

Interns must not reveal the identity of clients or any information that would uncover the identity without written permission from the clients. There are two exceptions to this principle. The first is if the clients may be dangerous to themselves or others, and the second is in cases of the abuse and neglect of children and the elderly. In these situations, interns are required to inform their supervisors, who will contact the proper agencies and authorities. In some instances, courts can order the release of case notes and records. Interns should also become familiar with state laws. Confidentiality must also be maintained in the classroom when sharing information from cases.

COMPETENCY

Interns must acknowledge the limitations of their abilities to assist clients. It is imperative that they accept that some situations are beyond their experience and obtain assistance from their agency supervisors and employees.

CORRUPTION

Interns must not be involved in any illegal operations or violations of laws. They should not take part in any attempt to undermine the criminal justice system or abuse the power, given by the state, associated with their internships. Interns have a duty to report any mismanagement of justice noticed while they are interning. They are obligated to treat all clients with justice and equity.

INTERPERSONAL RELATIONSHIPS

Interns will not develop a clinical relationship with anyone with whom they have an existing relationship of any type. It is unethical for interns to see classmates, co-workers, friends, or family members as clients. It is also unethical for them to become sexually or romantically involved with agency clients. Interns will not be involved in sexual harassment. I hereby agree to follow the guidelines stated above. I will also become familiar with the ethical guidelines for the professional discipline associated with the internship placement agency.

Signature of Intern_____ **Date**_____

Figure 10.1   Sample Ethical Agreement Form

Confidentiality

What is confidentiality? It is the principle that clients have the right to determine who will have access to information about them and their treatment and other privileged information, such as their criminal histories. In many mental health agencies, confidentiality is considered the primary ethical responsibility. However, the issues and limits of confidentiality vary from agency to agency.

As an intern, you will be expected to adhere to certain ethical guidelines for your benefit and protection, as well as those of clients, internship supervisors and agencies, and the internship coordinator and university. Whenever you have questions about ethical conduct, you should discuss them with your agency supervisor or internship coordinator.

If you are involved in counseling during your internship, your clients need to believe that their identities and the information they share will be released only with their permission (most agencies provide release-of-information forms for this purpose). Without this guarantee, clients are reluctant to express their thoughts and feelings openly. The only acceptable instances for breaching confidentiality are cases in which you have evidence that clients may be dangerous to themselves or others or are abusing or neglecting children or the elderly. In such situations, you should know your agency's policy and legal requirements for informing appropriate organizations. You need to become acquainted with particular legal proceedings that require case notes and other records to be released by order of the courts. If clients know that the courts can subpoena their records, they may be reluctant to share certain information, which may disrupt the treatment process (Nowell and Spruill, 1993). On the other hand, if clients are to make informed decisions, they should know the limits to confidentiality. Therefore, you must learn and follow the confidentiality policies of your agency and the laws of your state. When presenting and discussing case information in class, you must make sure that you maintain confidentiality. For instance, never use a client's name (or any other identifiable information) in written reports or oral presentations.

When interning at a criminal justice agency, you are responsible for inquiring about the issues and limits of confidentiality established by the agency and state laws. In this setting, you will probably be exposed to privileged information that you should not discuss outside the agency. For instance, if you are interning at a police department and are privileged to information regarding a raid, your discussion of it with friends, classmates, or family members may endanger the officers and jeopardize the raid. On the other hand, if you are interning in a state or federal prison, the policy on confidentiality or the state law may dictate that you must report certain information you receive, such as an escape that is being planned. If while you are interning as a probation officer, a client informs you that he or she has violated probation (for example, by leaving the state without permission), you should know if the policy on confidentiality requires that you inform your agency supervisor.

As an intern, it will not always be obvious to you how much of the information on clients you should share with your supervisor and co-workers. After orientation, whether you are given your own caseload or are sharing a co-worker's, you should ask your supervisor how much and what type of information on clients you need to share with the original caseworker, and even with the supervisor, before you begin to work with clients.

There has been an ongoing debate in the field regarding confidentiality. According to Clairborn et al. (1994), some studies have found that clients and the general public believe that confidentiality should never be breached. However, the respondents in Rubanowitz's (1987) study maintained that there are certain situations, usually involving knowledge of the possibility or actual commission of a crime, in which a client's confidentiality should be violated and appropriate authorities should be advised.

Of all the ethical and legal issues faced by helping professionals, confidentiality is the one that is most constantly considered a source of moral dilemmas (Pope and Vetter, 1992; Stadler and Paul, 1986). Because of the perceived significance of confidentiality and the frequency of moral dilemmas associated with it, you must fully understand its standards. In doing so, you will be able to avoid violating the standards through thoughtlessness.

The next sections discuss some general issues of confidentiality that apply to most clinical situations and criminal justice agencies. These issues are included only as general guidelines, so you must be certain that they can be helpful in your particular agency. If you are interning at an agency that serves minors, such as a juvenile detention facility, or a drug and alcohol treatment facility that practices group and/or family therapy, be aware that certain therapy techniques present unique issues and that these guidelines may not be appropriate to protect confidentiality in these settings (Paradise and Kirby, 1990; Vesper and Brock, 1990).

Release-of-Information Forms

Standard release-of-information forms to protect confidentiality are used by most agencies. (See Figure 10.2 for a sample form.) These are important forms that clients must sign before any written or verbal information about them can be released. The forms usually provide a place for listing the persons or organizations who are authorized to receive the information; the date of the release; the period during which the release of information is valid; the reason for the release; the precise details requested for release; the form of communication (written or verbal) for the release; the name of the client; the name of the person authorized to release the information (usually the therapist or supervisor); and finally, the signatures of the client and the therapist or supervisor (Bennett et al., 1990).

Customarily, if anyone contacts you by telephone or E-mail or visits you at the agency, declaring that he or she has the client's consent to discuss the client's case or see the client's files but is not listed on the release form (or the client has not signed a release form), you must not even admit that the person is a client, much less share the files or discuss the case. If the person is insistent, the best way to handle the situation without acknowledging that the person is a client is to say something like this: "I am unable to share any information that may be retained by this agency without written consent. I am sure you are aware of the importance of confidentiality, and I will be happy to assist you with whatever information I can once I receive a release of information."

If the person continues to demand information, you should refer him or her to your supervisor. Do not allow yourself to be pressured into providing *any* information without the release-of-information form.

This form authorizes the release and sharing of information
between_____
        (Intern's agency)

and_____
        (Organization requesting the information)

with regard to the client named below. The signing of this release form by the person/guardian allows the above-named agencies to share with each other relevant information about the client. This information is limited to referral information, psychological test reports, medical records, arrest records, and recommendations for treatment. It may be in the form of written reports or conversation in person or by telephone. This permission can be terminated—in writing or verbally—at any time by the client.

PLEASE *PRINT* THE NAME OF THE CLIENT_____

_____   _____
Client's Signature (Guardian)   Date

_____   _____
Authorized Signature (Supervisor)   Date

Figure 10.2   Sample Release-of-Information Form

Protecting Files

To protect files and guarantee the confidentiality of records, you should store all case notes and any other relevant information in *locked* file cabinets. It is good practice to keep cabinets locked any time you are away from their location, especially overnight. You should never leave your notes or any other records that identify clients where they may be accidentally seen by other agency employees or the general public. A supplementary safeguard used by many agencies is to stamp "Confidential" on all case records. If your agency has converted the paper files to computer files, you should never leave the computer screen on in your absence, thereby allowing others to gain access to the files.

If one of your assignments as an intern is to keep a journal, you should be careful not to lose or misplace it. As a precaution, I tell my interns who keep journals to mask the clients' identities by using fake names or initials. It is a good practice to avoid using only first names because of the possibility that they may be associated with actual clients.

Information Sharing among Co-workers

By now, it should be clear that no information should be shared with outside sources without a release-of-information form from your client. But what about sharing information with your co-workers? This issue of confidentiality is not as clear-cut. Baird (1996) suggested that before you share information on a client with another agency employee, you should ask yourself: Who is the person? Why does he (or she) want the information? What information is being requested? Where are you (public or private setting)? When should you discuss the information? How will you share the information?

(See Box 10.1.) Instant and spontaneous self-examination of these questions whenever you consider sharing information with co-workers may help you decrease the mistakes you may make in issues of confidentiality.

Abuse

Several state laws require health professionals and educators to report cases of suspected or known child abuse or neglect (Swenson, 1993), as well as cases of the neglect or abuse of elderly persons. As an intern, if you are working with a child or elderly person who informs you that he or she is being physically or sexually abused or if there is physical evidence that abuse has taken place, you are required to inform your supervisor, who, in turn, is obligated to inform the proper agencies or authorities. The agency that investigates claims and intercedes for the protection of the child is usually called Child Protective Services, a branch of the Department of Social Services in a city or county. The same department also investigates claims of elderly abuse and neglect.

In an extensive review of legal and clinical concerns connected with child neglect and abuse, Howing and Wodarski (1992) stated that because of the frequency of child abuse, it is probable that helping professionals will be confronted with instances of suspected abuse. Because the laws differ from state to state and because of vagueness in the law, it is sometimes difficult to know when to report.

Despite these difficulties, most states that require child neglect and abuse to be reported provide protection from civil liability (being sued) if the reports are submitted in good will and without animosity. Negligence in reporting, however, may result in criminal or civil lawsuits (Howing and Wodarski, 1992).

Thus, early in your internship, you should ask your supervisor to inform you about the agency's policy and the state law on reporting neglect and abuse. Be aware that the accusation of abuse is serious, and you should not be quick to report a case without investigating it (under agency supervision); nevertheless, if your supervisor thinks there are legitimate reasons, the abuse must be reported to the proper authorities. It would also be advisable to inform your internship coordinator that you have reported the incident to your agency supervisor.

Competence

During your internship training, you will need to monitor your ethical behavior continuously and deliberately. Doing so will help you operate at *your* level of competence—another important standard of most codes of ethics.

In time, you may become as skilled at performing some of the same tasks as your co-workers and may be viewed as more competent by your supervisor and agency employees. However, you may still face situations about which you are uncertain. Therefore, it is crucial for you to recognize the extent and limitations of your skills and ask for help from your supervisor when you need it. For example, a client who is contemplating suicide will not be within your ability to handle, no matter how much you may want to help the client, and must be reported to your supervisor immediately. Always be aware that good intentions cannot replace

Box 10.1   SHARING INFORMATION WITH COLLEAGUES

Guidelines for sharing information with outside sources are relatively clear and the rule can be summarized succinctly as "Not without written permission from the client." Questions about sharing information with colleagues within an internship placement are not as easily answered. As each setting and situation are different, it may be helpful to offer a general framework you can use to help make your decisions. This framework revolves around the "W" question words: who, why, what, where, when, and how. Before sharing information about a client with anyone, you should ask yourself:

1. Who is the person? Has the client given permission for them to have the information? What is their role or authority within the clinical setting? What professional training do they have? What is their relationship to the client? What do you think of their clinical skills, ethical knowledge, etc.? Also ask yourself if the other person knows about and respects the principle of confidentiality.

2. Why do they want the information? Are they involved in the client's treatment in some way? Are they just curious? Are they seeking information to help them understand the client, or are they likely to use it in a counterproductive way?

3. What information is being requested? Is the person asking for data such as address, phone, etc., or are they asking for clinical information about the nature of the client's concerns or background? Are they asking for general impressions from tests or interviews, or do they want specific scores or answers to specific questions? Remember that merely because someone is asking for a certain type of information does not mean that you should provide the information requested. Depending on the circumstances, you may choose to offer summaries or general impressions rather than specific test results or interview responses. You may also choose to offer no information at all if there is a probability that it will not be used responsibly and professionally.

4. Where are you? Is the setting private, or are you in a public place where others could easily overhear your discussion? Are the office doors closed? Could people in the waiting room hear you? Are other clients nearby?

5. When should you discuss the information? Is now the best time to share information? Will you have adequate time to discuss and explain things or will you be rushed and not do an adequate job? Would it be better to schedule a specific time and place rather than sharing things in passing?

6. How will you share the information? Is it best to discuss information directly one on one, or can you accomplish the task over the phone? Should you formalize the exchange of information in writing, either by providing the information itself in written form or by keeping notes of the conversation? What are the relative pros and cons of direct verbal versus written exchange?

If you ask these questions immediately and automatically each time you consider sharing information about a client, the chances of carelessness will be reduced significantly.

Source: Brian N. Bairn, Department of Psychology, Pacific Lutheran University, Tacoma, Washington, 1996.

competence and that there will be times when you will not be the best judge of your capabilities and behavior.

You may be unaware of several factors that must be weighed in evaluating specific situations, such as formal and informal agency policies (which are discussed in Chapter 8) or policies of other criminal justice agencies that must be considered. Consulting with your co-workers and supervisor is a good policy to follow, both during your internship and after you become a professional.

There are several reasons why clients are reassigned to other agency employees. Many times, the clients need special attention or specific services that are not immediately recognized, and your supervisor may have to assign them to workers who are more skilled in these particular areas. This happened with one of my interns, who felt much better when the supervisor advised him that the client needed the skills of a substance abuse counselor, which the intern did not have. The most important lesson you can learn during your internship is how much *you do not know*. This learning process will continue into your professional career, and you should never be too proud or ashamed to seek assistance. Even after several years of work experience, supervision will play a primary role in your professional training. After I received a master's degree in social work, I had to have five years of supervised training before I could apply for state certification, which would allow me to participate in unsupervised counseling. In addition, to keep state certification and maintain my practice as a family counselor, I had to have my case notes reviewed monthly by a certified social worker who had been practicing at least 10 years.

Because professionals recognize that there is always new information, and hence the need for continuous study, most states require some form of continuing education credits to obtain and maintain certification and licensing. In the criminal justice field, you will be expected continually to acquire knowledge by reading professional journals and attending various conferences related to your area of specialization and consult with other professionals with greater skills in that area.

In concluding this discussion of competence, I want to emphasize that interns are held responsible for their actions just as professionals are; it is this fact that interns do not always realize. For instance, one of my students who was working in child protective services was instructed by her supervisor to take an infant to a foster care home; instead, she took the infant to her home overnight and was charged with kidnapping. Her supervisor and I, as her internship coordinator, could also have been held responsible for the intern's actions. However, we were not, and with our support, she was placed on probation, but not allowed to complete her internship with the agency. This student, acting in a professional role and given primary responsibility for the infant's care, should have been aware that it was her responsibility to follow the same legal and ethical standards as those of a professional (Zakutansky and Sirles, 1993).

One of the basic rules I stress with my students regarding their levels of competence is "Do no harm." It is natural for you to want to accept challenges, appreciating that your success will increase your confidence, elevate your self-esteem, and improve your skills. But this need must be secondary; your primary concern must be the consequences of your actions for your clients.

Corruption

Although it is unlikely that you will be involved in situations in which you must deal with corruption as an intern, it is possible that you may encounter corruption, since this issue has been considered a frequent problem for the criminal justice system. Corruption occurs when a person uses his or her official position to obtain personal profit. In some cases, interns work (as you may do) in an official role that is formally defined by the agency's organizational structure. During the years of my program, only one student reported being involved in corruption. He said: "While on a ride-along, I observed a suspect confess to stealing several season ticket packages for sports events. Before booking the suspect, the arresting officers 'pocketed the tickets.' Later they offered me a package and I accepted because I was afraid to refuse."

Obviously, this is a clear-cut example of corruption. But sometimes the issue is not so clear. For example, while interning, would you be comfortable accepting free meals or free passes to musical or sports events or other gifts? Even though your agency may not provide clear-cut policies regarding these and similar situations, they may fit into the ethically gray area of corruption. In such cases, your value system will influence your response. However, it will not always be easy to adhere to your value system when your peers pressure you to overlook your values. For example, as a police intern, you may be determined never to be involved in police brutality, but when invited by your supervisor or other officers to participate, you may find that your need for acceptance may come into conflict with your values. One of my interns was confronted with a similar situation. Because his value system would not allow him to participate, he felt he would be evaluated unfairly by his supervisor and alienated by other officers, so he requested and received a transfer to another agency. At all times, you must keep in mind that you are learning to be a professional, and as an intern, you will occasionally make mistakes and use poor judgment. These mistakes can be minimized, however, if you have frequent discussions with your peers, agency supervisor, and internship coordinator.

Dual Relationships

If, as an intern, you are providing counseling, professional ethics forbid the establishment of *dual relationships*. Boryrs and Pope (1989) and Kitchener (1988) reported that even though dual relationships include a broad range of interactions, the underlying ethical standard and primary concern is that as a counselor, you must avoid any involvement with your client that could jeopardize the healing process. For example, functioning as a counselor for another intern at your agency would be considered a dual relationship. An even more serious and damaging form of dual relationship would be your involvement in a romantic or sexual relationship with your client. This issue is addressed later in the chapter.

Kagle and Giebelhausen (1994) and Baird (1996) noted that the risk involved in dual relationships is the probability that counselors may, intentionally or unintentionally, allow some facet of their nonprofessional relationships to disrupt their counseling relationships. Gutheil and Gabbard (1993) pointed out that what may initially be seen as a slight departure from usual procedures may eventually lead to more significant violations.

In some instances, clients have been responsible for initiating dual relationships. If you are ever confronted with this situation, it is your responsibility to handle the matter in an ethical manner. The best rule for avoiding dual relationships is never to provide counseling for anyone with whom you share an existing relationship.

As an intern, when associating with agency clients and co-workers, you should conduct yourself in a professional manner, which will help you develop and maintain appropriate relationships. Avoid the temptation to begin a personal relationship with a client outside the agency because the situation could lead to circumstances that may cause you to compromise your values and ethics. One of my interns, working in a federal prison camp without a fence and with open access to the roadway, assisted an inmate who was slipping out for the night, with the intention of returning before morning roll call, by giving him a ride to the nearest bar. When the intern was released from her placement, she stated: "He was already out; I just gave him a lift." Of course, that was the end of that internship. The issue that concerned both me and her field supervisor was that she felt she had done nothing to warrant her release from the placement. In this case the intern obviously developed a personal relationship with the inmate that clouded her values and had a negative impact on her professional conduct. With all the media attention on unethical romantic and sexual conduct, it should be obvious that these relationships are the most harmful and legally significant models of dual relationships. The ethical codes of all helping professional organizations specially forbid sexual relations with clients (Kagle and Giebelhausen, 1994); nevertheless, these relationships continue to occur. The neglect of this standard has created much trouble for many professionals, tremendous stress for their families, and severe and permanent harm to the people they desired to help.

Another situation is when an intern consents to a sexual relationship with an agency supervisor. Who is guilty of sexual misconduct? The agency supervisor is in the role of mentor and role model and usually grades the intern. Because of the unequal distribution of power in this relationship, the intern's consent to participate in unethical activities does not relieve the supervisor of responsibility for unprofessional actions (Walsh, 1990). If you are approached by an agency employee, there are several creative ways of dealing with these sexual advances. One that has worked for other interns is to tell the person that the professional code of ethics prohibits intimacy between interns and co-workers.

In addition to professional organizations' codes of ethics, several states also have laws regarding sexual misconduct that make it not only an ethical issue, but a criminal matter, such as the example of sexual harassment given above (Strasburger et al., 1991). After reviewing the existing laws, Applebaum (1990) reported that in many instances the breach of this ethical standard is considered a felony and may result in imprisonment and fines. There is also little protection from civil lawsuits (Jorgenson et al., 1991).

JUSTICE, EQUALITY, AND PUNISHMENT

Whatever occurs at your internship placement, recognize it as one experience. Do not judge all agencies, employees, clients, or yourself by this limited experience. Valuable lessons can be learned from even the worst environments, from the most trying clients, and the most unhealthy staff members. You may, indeed, have experiences during your internship that may disappoint or distress you. However, this is not a good reason to quit the internship or conclude that it is not a good learning experience.

While you are interning as a student of criminal justice, criminology, or related courses, your classroom experience, academic assignments, and the media will influence the formation of your values regarding the criminal justice system. Your comprehension derived from these experiences will be exposed to the realities of the administration of justice and of the people who are administering this justice.

Your internship is the time when you will anticipate transferring theory into practice. On some occasions, however, you may think that what was presented in the classroom does not apply to the *real world* of the criminal justice system. I mentioned earlier that one of my interns witnessed a case of police brutality. He wanted to report it, but did not, and asked to be transferred to another agency. This was his first encounter with the reality that unjust and unfair administration of justice by *professionals* in the criminal justice system does exist. Therefore, in some cases, their actions may be detrimental to clients, their agency, and you if it meets their needs. Another intern of mine, while working as a legal assistant at the Office of the State Attorney, was infuriated to learn the extent to which plea bargaining was applied to felony cases (assault, rape, battery, etc.). After assisting and observing the attorney commit so many hours to case presentations and involvement in plea bargaining, at the end of the internship she decided not to apply to law school. The lesson she learned was that even well-intentioned programs, as plea bargaining was created to be, run by healthy, caring people, do not always work efficiently or properly. Many times, the greatest efforts by the most considerate people are obstructed by faulty programs. These are two examples of the fact that the administration of justice is not always honorable or equitable. As an intern you may be exposed to what the profession considers bargain and street justice. Involvement in these situations will usually create ethical or moral predicaments with which you must grapple. You will be confronted with how to deal with the situations, and you will examine your responsibility in them.

Although there are no cut-and-dried rules on how to handle unjust and unfair situations, it is suggested that you not interefere at the scene for fear that you might magnify a potentially dangerous situation. It is also recommended that you discuss the situation with your internship coordinator for assistance managing the same or a similar situation.

If you become disturbed by an immoral or unlawful situation, first discuss it with your internship coordinator, who will help you decide whether to take the issue to your agency supervisor or co-worker. In any event, be aware that your internship may be in jeopardy if you decide to confront a co-worker or your agency supervisor.

My students have received mixed responses to their reports of unethical or illegal incidences. Whereas some reports have been well received, others have not, and the consequences have been negative. For example, one intern, observing a co-worker making frequent trips to the rest room, thought the person was ill and followed her in. She discovered the co-worker taking drugs and reported the incident to her agency supervisor, even though she thought she might be ostracized by her fellow employees. Because this was a drug-free workplace, however, the agency supervisor and the other employees appreciated her report about the employee who was acting in an unprofessional and illegal way. On the other hand, another intern working in a correctional facility was ostracized by his fellow employees when he reported an incident of sexual misconduct between an inmate and a staff member.

Even though the issues of justice, equity, and punishment must be addressed, most interns gain a strong sense of accomplishment and satisfaction from their internships. They enjoy the opportunity to work with remarkable clients and to encounter healthy, caring professionals whom they come to admire and are pleased with their work and their learning experience, as you will be.

SUMMARY

Your personal values greatly influence your loyalty to the ethical guidelines of the criminal justice system. To be an asset to the criminal justice system while interning, you must understand your own value system and accept different values held by your clients and agency staff members. You must be open to learning more about yourself and evaluating and reevaluating your values. You should never sacrifice your values to establish good rapport with your peers, co-workers, or agency supervisor.

Ethical guidelines exist to safeguard the well-being of clients, professionals, and professions. As an intern, it is your responsibility to be well informed about the ethical standards instituted by your profession and the agency in which you are interning and to discuss them with your agency supervisor and internship coordinator. In this chapter we have examined important ethical issues that are relevant to you as an intern.

During your internship, you may witness incidences in which clients are being treated unjustly and unfairly. You may also observe co-workers and/or supervisors involved in immoral and illegal activities. These situations exist, and you will be affected by the ethical dilemmas they create. Learning how to deal appropriately with these difficulties is a crucial part of your learning experience and your professional development.

Evaluation and Future Careers

Now that you know the various aspects of field placements, such as your role as an intern, the roles of the faculty coordinator and the agency supervisor, and the importance of values and ethical standards, it is time to assess your internship experience, to think of your future career, and to use the resource guide located in the back of this book to locate and contact several criminal justice agencies in 25 major cities in the United States.

The following chapters will help you evaluate your internship experience and set future career goals. Chapter 11 will assist you in evaluating your total field educational experience, and in Chapter 12 we provide invaluable information regarding your professional future in the career field or graduate education. They also discuss several things that you have to do to complete your internship relationships with your supervisor, peers, and other co-workers.

Now that you are near the end of your internship, a significant component of the procedure for terminating your field placement is the review process that you and your field supervisor undergo. In this process, you and your supervisor should allot adequate time to discuss your personal and professional development and any areas in which you need additional work.

Evaluation of Field Education Experience

Questions for Students

Did you make the desired progress on your original internship goals?

What strengths and weaknesses did you discover during your field experience?

How has this experience influenced your future goals?

EVALUATION OF PERSONAL AND PROFESSIONAL PROGRESS

The traditional way to measure your progress is filling out some type of evaluation form, as discussed in Chapter 9. Although your internship coordinators have probably asked that these reports be sent directly to them to help them determine your grades, you and your agency supervisor should first review these reports and jointly discuss your views and opinions. In our program, three seminars are scheduled during the semester. The purpose of the first meeting is for the interns to become acquainted with each other and the internship coordinator and for the internship coordinator to provide a syllabus and direction for the course during the semester. At the second (midterm) meeting, the interns share their experiences with their placements, and they discuss their midterm evaluations and progress to date received from the agency supervisors. The third meeting again focuses on shared experiences and group and individual discussions of the final evaluations and progress toward the interns' goals for personal and professional growth. In addition, weekly informal individual sessions are held to discuss goals and learning objectives, which provide more clear-cut areas for evaluating the field experiences. At these meetings, the interns take notes to assist them with their final self-evaluations.

The hardest part of the evaluation process is probably learning to accept critical feedback effectively. It is natural for you to want to hear only compliments and praise from your coordinator and supervisor, and they would prefer to give you glowing evaluations. Although praise is important because it increases your self-esteem and gives you the strength and faith to persevere, constructive criticism is vital because it establishes essential directions for further personal and professional development. Therefore, it is recommended that you welcome constructive criticism as a means of identifying and setting future goals. Bairn (1966) suggested that one way to learn to accept criticism constructively is to write a self-evaluation in which you identify things you did well during your internship and areas in which you recognize that you need to improve. This exercise will help you see your strengths and weaknesses before the joint review and better accept and process critical feedback. Furthermore, self-evaluation can become a regular practice of personal reflection that will be useful throughout your career.

It is important to record carefully, for later reflection, how much you have changed personally and professionally during your internship. If you keep a journal, as suggested in Chapter 7, you will have evidence to support your intuitive feeling of having gained a great deal. During your internship, several factors have interacted to help you accomplish the goals and objectives that you set out to gain from your field education experience, and your initial impressions of your internship experience are significant for assessing your personal growth and professional progress. For instance, your peers', agency supervisors', and co-workers' expectations of you can be crucial assessment factors. Your internship may have been the first opportunity you have had to satisfy the expectations of experts in your desired profession. Assessing how well you have met others' expectations, as well as your own, is an important part of self-evaluation.

FIELD SUPERVISOR'S EVALUATION

Interns are usually evaluated by both their agency supervisors and faculty internship coordinators according to criteria they receive before their internships began. In our program, agency supervisors give students this information during initial interviews in the semester before the internships take place, and (as the faculty internship coordinator) I give them a syllabus containing my requirements and evaluation criteria in the first seminar meeting during the first week of their internships. (See Chapter 9 for a sample syllabus and criteria for the required term paper.) Although expectations and requirements may vary, there are some common areas of evaluation.

Most agency supervisors' expectations are based on their experiences with interns and facilitating the personal and professional development of other agency employees. These expectations are usually broad based because the experiences and expectations of internships are different and the personal goals of interns vary.

At the beginning of your internship, you should ask your faculty internship coordinator or agency supervisor if there are established guidelines for evaluation; if there are, you should review the guidelines immediately to make sure that you understand what is expected of you. It has been my experience that some agencies, particularly those that are implementing their first internship programs, do not have an established format for evaluation. Consequently, I automatically give the interns I supervise a broad-based sample of a fixed-format evaluation during our first seminar meeting. If your supervisor does not have a fixed format for evaluation, review the sample evaluation presented in Chapter 9. Here are some specific areas that most supervisors are concerned about:

1. Reliability and dependability
2. Ethical knowledge and behavior
3. Level of knowledge and learning ability
4. Receptiveness to supervision
5. Interaction with clients
6. Socialization with co-workers
7. Workmanship
8. Aptitude for the profession

Reliability and Dependability   Your supervisor will evaluate you on such things as dress, punctuality, attendance, constructive use of time, completion of assignments, and completion of required internship hours.

Ethical Knowledge and Behavior   Your supervisor will probably inform you of the agency's ethical guidelines. As an intern, you will be expected to develop (or already have) knowledge of general ethical guidelines, know the ethical guidelines of the agency, demonstrate your insights into and sensitivity for ethical concerns, and display personal conduct compatible with ethical guidelines. (See Chapter 10 for ethical principles in the field.)

Level of Knowledge and Learning Ability   You will be evaluated on your knowledge of the client population at the beginning and end of your internship and on your ability to learn and process new information and apply new information in your agency setting.

Receptiveness to Supervision   You will be evaluated on how receptive you are to feedback and recommendations from your supervisor and your active participation in obtaining the required supervision. Again, your willingness to explore personal strengths and weaknesses will be weighed, as will the effectiveness of your implementation of your supervisor's recommendations.

Interaction with Clients   Your ability to interact well with clients is an important consideration. The criteria will include your level of comfort while interacting with clients, how effectively you communicate during interactions, and your sensitivity to clients' needs and cultural and gender differences.

Socialization with Co-workers   The ability to be relaxed while interacting with other agency personnel, to communicate effectively while relating information and verbalizing your views, and to obtain information and opinions from your co-workers are important aspects of your professional development and meaningful elements for evaluation.

Workmanship   The quality of your performance in keeping credible and precise records; in maintaining reliable, factually correct, and professionally composed reports; and in presenting articulate verbal narratives that are administratively useful will have a strong influence on your evaluation.

Aptitude for the Profession   The caliber of your overall accomplishments during your internship and the extent of your personal and professional growth will contribute greatly to assessments of your aptitude for working in your profession. At the conclusion of the internship, you and your supervisor may determine that you are a good candidate for working in the field represented by the agency. On the other hand, the experience may cause you to rethink your professional goals and to begin to pursue other areas. Some of my students have stated that they would rather find out at this time in their lives that they need to change career paths rather than to make this discovery after completing their degrees. Therefore, be aware that one important purpose of an internship is to discover where *you do not wish to work*, as well as where you do.

FIELD-SITE EVALUATION

As part of their internship assignments, my students are required to assess their agencies on the basis of how well the agencies met their internship goals. Some students have also evaluated agencies on how well the agencies' goals and objectives were met, on the basis of the discussion in Chapter 6. Even though your faculty coordinator will make site visits, it is impossible to know how conducive the internship experience is to your desired educational outcome. For this reason, your faculty coordinator will be interested in your opinions about how well the agency met your expectations and goals and whether future interns should be placed there. This evaluation will also benefit you in the future when you consider employment opportunities. One intern evaluated the placement site this way:

> Overall I really enjoyed my experience as an intern. In my agency [Federal Bureau of Prisons], I learned about the behind-the-scenes part of criminal justice. I didn't have any hands-on experience with inmates. Since my office deals with the paperwork, not with the inmates themselves, I could not really see how most of the criminological theories I learned in class applied in the real world. I could not see how programs affect the inmates or why the inmates may have committed the crimes. It is hard to understand these things when you never actually meet the inmates....

I wish to state that I have enjoyed other aspects of this experience. I have learned a lot and made some valuable contacts in the criminal justice system. I would recommend this internship to anyone who wants to learn about the behind-the-scenes part of criminal justice. It would be especially valuable for someone who is interested in community corrections. However, I would not recommend this internship to someone who wants hands-on experience.

This was a first-time placement, and this brief statement helped me determine the type of students who would benefit from it. The following statement by another intern indicates that even though the agency lacked sufficient resources, the placement was beneficial:

As a result of my internship placement with the Guardian Ad Litem Program, my criminological understanding has been greatly clarified and challenged in terms of actual criminal justice-related work. I was able to to observe first hand things that I only read about in textbooks and to participate in judicial court proceedings, which gave me the experience of seeing the manner in which a judge in delinquency proceedings reaches certain rulings. I also noticed the different styles and attitudes that the judges brought to their roles and how they affected their decisions and the behavior of other agency workers....

Several flaws were also evident in and around the agency. The main flaw was the computer system network. For an agency that has between 28 and 83 workers a day, only five computers were available. One computer is usually not even open for use on a regular basis. Also, audio and video equipment, which is necessary for training sessions, is either outdated or experiences many operational difficulties. However, these flaws are not enough to offset the overall positive experience. The GAL program is, in my opinion, of superior quality given the number of workers and volunteers it has. It truly makes a difference in the lives of children.

As an intern, you may be hesitant to share your opinions with agency staff; however, your impressions are usually appreciated because they bring a new outlook to the issues.

FACULTY COORDINATOR'S EVALUATION

During your internship, your faculty coordinator might pay two to three site visits to your agency, depending on the number of interns placed for the semester. These visits, which are usually spread throughout the semester (beginning, midterm, and end), although informative, do not provide ample opportunity for field evaluations. Consequently, the faculty coordinator's evaluation is determined largely by the field supervisor's evaluations. Some faculty coordinators may supplement their evaluation criteria, as I do, with a required observation-participation term paper.

Because of the restrictions on actual observation, your faculty coordinator may evaluate and grade you on the basis of his or her personal standards applied to interns; your participation in seminars and weekly informal discussions; your journal entries; the quality of your term paper, if applicable; and your field supervisor's evaluation.

Some students have informed me that they have been asked to evaluate their agency supervisors and to suggest ways in which the supervisory process could be improved. If this request is made of you, realize that the process not only helps your supervisor but allows you to practice giving sincere feedback. The reciprocal exchange of opinions can be beneficial to both you and your supervisor in bringing better closure to your relationship and the internship. If you are given this opportunity, remember the earlier discussion on giving and receiving constructive criticism. Also because of the authority your supervisor has over you, you must consider carefully whether to articulate any negative statements to your supervisor. The University of Miami has eliminated this problem for students in evaluating all faculty by requiring that the evaluation process be completed in the absence of faculty and the results withheld until after the grading period.

RELATING THE FIELD EXPERIENCES TO FUTURE CAREERS

Many colleges and universities have career planning and placement centers with high-quality resources to help students attain future career goals relative to internship experiences, whether the goal is to find a full-time job upon graduation or to attend graduate school. An effective career planning process begins on your first day on campus and continues throughout your college years, including your internship, if you take advantage of the numerous workshops, panel discussions, career fairs, and presentations of information presented by on-campus recruiters. Being an active participant in these events will afford you the knowledge and opportunity to connect your internship experience to your future career.

SUMMARY

This chapter focused on the evaluation process, and we discussed how to measure your personal growth and professional development during your internship. It also described how your field supervisor and faculty internship coordinator appraise you and gave some insight into how you may appraise your internship site.

Assessments by your field supervisor and faculty coordinator are reliable indicators of your personal and professional growth, as well as your potential as a criminal justice professional. Furthermore, some supervisors think feedback should be bilateral and encourage interns to give their honest opinions on the ways that supervision can be enhanced in the future. If you are afforded this opportunity, remember that there is a natural imbalance in the authoritative arrangement of the supervisor–intern relationship, so you should consider carefully voicing any negative opinions to your supervisor.

Evaluating your experiences should be a continuous process and should not just occur when you leave the agency at the end of your internship. A detailed evaluation of your internship experiences will make them more meaningful. Self-evaluation, honestly appraising your accomplishments, is one of the most meaningful skills that you can cultivate during your internship because it will contribute greatly to your future growth and development in whatever profession you enter after college.

c h a p t e r   1 2

Future Careers

Questions for Students

What kind of job do you want?

How would you plan a job search?

Do you plan to attend professional school?

PREPARING TO CHOOSE

Most students who take criminal justice internships are usually interested in careers in such disciplines as the law, law enforcement, corrections, and juvenile justice. While interning and after your placement has ended, you will be confronted with decisions regarding your future career goals. To make these decisions, you will need to ask yourself several questions, such as these: Was the workplace conducive to being productive? Did I enjoy working with the clients? Would I want to continue working in the same type of agency? Do I have the credentials, or am I willing to obtain the credentials, needed to obtain a position with the agency? These are only a few of the many questions you will need to consider to set realistic career goals. These questions indicate that there are several steps that you must take in setting your careers goals: (1) discovering the types of positions that are appropriate for your skills, (2) locating those positions, (3) composing a résumé that will entice people to employ you, (4) obtaining interviews, (5) preparing for interviews, and (6) determining whether particular positions and organizations will contribute to your personal and professional growth. In this chapter we provide some information that will help you consider these and other factors related to obtaining a position in your chosen field.

DETERMINING VOCATIONAL ASPIRATIONS

The first step in determining your vocational aspirations is to find out what kind of job you want. When making this decision, consider that the work you choose should be interesting and challenging, should make use of your professional skills and abilities, and should provide educational opportunities for professional growth. The first step in finding out what kind of job you want is to take a personal assessment of yourself. In this assessment you should consider your personal likes and dislikes and how important maximum job satisfaction is to you. You should also evaluate your skills, such as writing skills and interpersonal skills. Another important consideration is where you want to live. What climate do you prefer, and would you rather live and work in an urban or a rural community? The answers to these and other questions that you ask yourself will point you in the right direction for finding the kind of job you want.

To conduct a personal assessment you should make a list of factors that are necessary for you to experience satisfaction and contentment in a job. Finance is the first important area to consider:

- Will you have to repay college loans after graduation?
- What are your financial requirements regarding housing, transportation, and family support (if applicable)?
- How much money do you want to make in the future?

Next consider your personal preferences:

- Do your like working alone, or interacting with others?
- Do you enjoy working on computers?
- How much supervision do you prefer?
- Do you like assisting others in dealing with and solving their problems?
- How much job-related traveling do you want to do?
- Would you consider job training that required long periods away from your family?
- Are you interested in graduate education to help you advance to a supervisory or executive position?

The second important area to consider is your abilities and deficiencies related to the skills required for your chosen discipline. Among the questions you should ask yourself are the following:

- Are you relaxed when interacting with others?
- Is it easy for you to socialize or converse with people from different social and ethnic–racial backgrounds?

- Are you a self-starter with leadership abilities?
- Are you good at creating ideas and managing projects?
- Are you research oriented and computer literate?
- Are you able to identify and solve problems?
- Are you deadline conscious, or do you procrastinate?
- How well do you work under pressure?

The answers to these and other questions should give you a fairly good perception of your skills and help you match them to the requirements for your desired field. The third important area to consider is job requirements that you may not be able to fulfill that have no bearing on your skills, such as things you cannot or will not do because they conflict with your moral code. For example, if you are considering a job in law enforcement, could you actually shoot someone? Do you believe in capital punishment? If not, could you be involved in sending someone to prison who might be executed? The fourth important area to consider is the effects of your internship, especially these two questions: Did skills improve during your internship? Did your internship experience verify that the field you wish to enter is the right one for you, or did it convince you to seek a different career path? Use this discussion to assist you in determining the types of jobs that will suit your particular combination of skills and interests, as well as any additional training you wish to pursue.

The final area to consider is geographic location. The necessary questions for this important element are these:

- Do you want to stay in your hometown or state?
- Are you willing to relocate? If so, to what area?
- Do you prefer a warm, cold, or temperate climate?
- Do you prefer urban, suburban, or rural living?
- Can you afford to live in the geographic area that you prefer?

The answers to these questions and others will be helpful in determining whether your career choices are accessible in your desired geographic location.

Two tools are available to assist you in determining the types of employment that may suit you: the *Encyclopedia of Careers and Vocational Guidance* and the *Occupational Outlook Handbook*, both of which can be found in the reference section of most libraries. The encyclopedia is in four volumes. Volume 1 describes a wide range of professions. Each entry contains an overview of the profession, including career opportunities, educational requirements, and philosophy. Volumes 2, 3, and 4 present detailed information on several hundred professions, including a brief history, nature of the work, working conditions, requirements, opportunities for education and exploration, techniques for entry and advancement, and information on earnings. The handbook, a smaller version of the encyclopedia, includes information on over 200 careers and affords the same details. Both guides provide information on conventional and mainstream jobs and various unusual ones, but the handbook describes more criminal justice-related occupations such as corrections officers.

Now that you have a fairly good perception of the type of job you want to obtain, you are ready to update or prepare your résumé.

PREPARING THE RÉSUMÉ

Whether you are updating your résumé or preparing one for the first time, you may feel frustrated attempting to compose a one-page marketing tool that will provide a good first impression of you to a complete stranger. Many of my students have shared their frustration with me, and the experience has been even more distressing for those who have not participated in extracurricular activities or held any part-time summer jobs because the purpose of a résumé is to obtain interviews, but until they are interviewed, prospective employers will judge them only by how they present themselves in their résumés. My advice to them, as it is to you, is that there are several types of résumés that will represent you in such a way that employers will want to interview you. You can use the instructions presented here as a guide, but a great deal will depend on your ability to portray your experiences distinctly, concisely, and impressively and produce a high-quality marketing product.

Basic Instructions

1. Usually, human resource personnel take a minute or less to study résumés, so your résumé must be well organized, legible, well written, and must highlight your special qualities. The career center staff at your school can help you write your résumé, and there are commercial services that will write your résumé for a fee. However, I recommend that you prepare your own résumé because you will be more familiar with the information you wish to convey and hence will be more comfortable during an interview. Furthermore, professionally prepared résumés cause interviewers to question their contents and create the impression that you lack the skills required to represent yourself in writing. You should use a résumé service only as a last resort if you cannot obtain assistance from any other resources mentioned here.

2. Be brief. Use short, clear, and informative sentences. Most employers prefer one-page résumés, which are usually sufficient for college graduates' experiences. It is not unusual to have to prepare several drafts before you are satisfied with the finished product.

3. The educational, work-experience, school, and community-involvement sections will provide the most positive impression of you as a candidate, so begin your résumé with the section that is most impressive and will more likely pique the reader's curiosity about you.

4. *Do not include negative information!* This is not a time to discuss your deficiencies, only your strong points. Remember that you are marketing

yourself, and although your résumé should be accurate, it should also be selective. The goal is to make yourself as attractive as possible.

5. Finally, *never* send out a résumé without having it critiqued by someone. The preferable person to show your résumé to is your internship coordinator. However, if for some reason you do not respect his or her writing skills, show it to the career planning or writing center staff at your university, or if all else fails, contact an instructor in the English Department. For the contents of two different types of résumés, see the samples in figures 3.2 and 3.3.

INVESTIGATING EMPLOYMENT OPPORTUNITIES

Your internship may be the initial introduction to the professional field of your choice. At the beginning of the internship, you should become attentive to professional opportunities that may be available to you later because of this experience. You can learn about career opportunities, entry-level processes, and qualifications for positions at your agency upon graduation by questioning your internship supervisor and co-workers. During your internship, you may also be able to investigate employment opportunities with other agencies and organizations that interact with your agency. For example, while one student was interning at a residential treatment facility for juvenile delinquents, she discovered that the Juvenile Assessment Center was interviewing for caseworkers. She interviewed, was accepted for the position, and is currently working at that center. Several of my students have learned about jobs this way, and others have been hired by their internship agencies. Thus, even if you are unable to obtain a position with your host agency, you have a good opportunity during your internship to network with professional contacts in the criminal justice field that you have made during your internship.

Before you complete your internship, I suggest that you get your supervisors' and co-workers' consent to list them as references on employment applications. Although it is not illegal to use someone's name as a reference without his or her permission, it is customary to do so. It is also appropriate to request a letter of recommendation from your supervisor, which should include the period of the internship, your responsibilities, your ability to perform those responsibilities, and his or her opinion of your candidacy for a position in the agency's discipline. Because these letters can be extraordinarily significant, you should give considerable thought to requesting them and observe specific fundamental courtesies to make the supervisor's work as simple as possible.

Before you request a letter of recommendation, be sure that you did the best work possible during your internship, as evidenced by the midterm and final evaluations prepared by your agency supervisor and internship coordinator. If you think or your evaluations have determined that your work has not been of the highest quality, you may want to ask your supervisor in person if he or she will write a positive recommendation for you. Even when you think your work deserves a positive recommendation, it is a good idea to mention your specific goals when requesting a letter because whereas your supervisor may feel awkward supporting some of your vocational aspirations, he or she may be comfortable writing a recommendation for a specific job or graduate program.

Once you have obtained permission to use your supervisors and co-workers as references and acquired letters of recommendation, you will be ready either to prepare or update your résumé, including your internship experience, any other additional part-time employment, and extracurricular activities. If your professional objective has been influenced by your internship experience, this change should be shown in your updated résumé. For example, Mandi, the student mentioned in the sample résumé in Chapter 3, was unhappy with her internship training and wanted more hands-on experience. If Mandi decided to seek part-time summer employment in the same field, she would need to include her desire to be involved in hands-on activities with clients in her professional objectives. She would also add, under relevant courses, "Internship with the Bureau of Prisons, Community Corrections Division," and state the duties she performed.

The cover letter that accompanies the résumé is the final document you need to prepare. The cover letter gives the prospective employer the first impression of you. Make sure that it is a basic, well-prepared letter with no erasures or strikeovers. In it, you should introduce yourself as a recent graduate who majored or minored in criminal justice; indicate your area of interest, such as juvenile delinquency or law enforcement; mention your internship education; and state why you are interested in the specific job for which you are applying. If you do not own a personal computer (PC), use one at the school library, and copy the cover letter onto a disk on which you can make changes based on the various positions for which you will apply. See Figure 3.4 for a sample cover letter.

Once your cover letter, résumé, and letters of recommendation are completed, you have received information on employment opportunities from your supervisors and co-workers, and obtained guidance from the university's career placement and planning center, your next step is to explore other key sources. These sources may include the Internet, contacts made through networking, classified advertisements in daily newspapers and professional journals, state and federal employment agencies, and the U.S. government.

The newest source of information about employment opportunities is the Internet. If you have a PC and modem, access to the Internet through companies such as Prodigy or American Online, and software, such as Netscape or Mosaic, that enables you to "surf" the Internet, you can gain access to a wealth of information in this area. If you do not have a PC or access to the Internet, most universities' career planning and placement centers do, and the staff will be happy to assist you in your search. There are several sites on the World Wide Web that provide information about investigating employment, that catalog employment opportunities throughout the country, and that allow you to list your résumé. The two that I am familiar with are CareerMosiac, <http://www.careermosic.com>, and Yahoo! Classifieds, <http://classifieds.yahoo.com>. You can learn about additional sites at your school's career center and the library.

Networking with your internship coordinator, other faculty members, class-mates, other acquaintances, and relatives can be beneficial in your job search. Your internship coordinator and other members of the criminal justice faculty are excellent resources because their networking relationships in the profession keep them informed of available positions in the field. Make a list of other people you know who work in the field of your choice or who know someone who does, contact these persons, and ask them for tips. Also ask them to circulate your résumé and get their permission to contact them periodically.

Of the resources mentioned, newspapers are the least beneficial because they carry few advertisements for criminal justice positions. However, it is still advisable to get the Sunday edition of the major newspaper in your area that devotes an entire section to classified advertisement. If you are interested in living and working in a particular city, it will be helpful to subscribe to that city's Sunday newspaper as well. Even though the information may be two to three days old by the time you receive the news-paper, it will be an indicator of the types of positions that are available and the deadlines for applying for them. Professional journals in criminal justice and related fields can be found in your university's library.

Advertisements for civil service positions are usually located on bulletin boards in state, county, and federal buildings and employment offices. Most of these positions require written examinations, and the details on the examinations are included in these notices. Information on the geographic locations and salaries of jobs are also provided, so you can compare your career goals with available positions. If you are interested in employment with the U.S. government, your local telephone directory will list the Federal Job Information Center in your area.

Interviewing

Now that your cover letter and résumé have gotten you an interview with an agency in a community that you feel is right for you, the next step is to become as knowledgeable as you can about the agency and the community before the interview. After you get this additional information, your task will be to sell yourself to the agency. During your interview, employers will be interested in your appearance, demeanor, communication skills, educational background, employment experiences, and long-term goals.

Appearance

Your appearance is usually the first criterion by which you are judged during an inter-view. The interviewer has his or her personal standards of appearance, along with any the agency may require, that you must meet during the interview. It is always safe to wear a traditional, conservative outfit to the interview:

- *Men:*   A dark suit, a white shirt, a striped or softly designed tie, black dress shoes, a dark overcoat, and a touch of cologne, if any. If you live in a warm climate, it is appropriate to eliminate the suit jacket and overcoat.

- *Women:*   A dark suit is still preferred, although off-white, beige, and tan suits are becoming more acceptable in warm climates. A white blouse, solid-color coordinating scarf (if desired), pumps, and hosiery are a must.

Briefcases are recommended because they give the appearance of professionalism. For additional information on dressing for the interviews, see Chapter 3.

Demeanor

The interviewer will learn a great deal about you from your demeanor (body language). Is your facial expression open and friendly, or do you look "mad at the world"? Body language is impressive, and although it is nonverbal, it communicates important information to the interviewer about your confidence and attention span. The following are a few ways to make it work in your favor:

1. Upon meeting your interviewer, make eye contact, smile, and give a strong handshake when introducing yourself. Since we live in a multicultural society, it is wise to learn the interviewer's background and customs, when possible, so that you do not send the wrong messages with your body language. For example, in some cultures and religions, men do not shake hands with women.
2. Present good posture by walking, standing, and sitting straight. When sitting, do not lean forward or cross your arms in a threatening or hostile position, but sit in an open, unguarded position. Folding your hands in your lap is quite appropriate.
3. Be and look attentive. Do not squirm, tap your fingers, or fiddle with jewelry or your hair.

Communication Skills

Speak with enthusiasm. Without overdoing it, show some excitement about the possibility of working in this aspect of your chosen career. Be aware of the following techniques and role-play the interview with someone to practice your communication skills prior to the interview:

1. Organize your thoughts into logical sentences and verbalize them clearly and grammatically.
2. When answering questions, be precise; offer sufficient information to answer the questions, saying neither too much nor too little. There are times when yes or no answers are necessary, but interviewers usually want you to give more extensive answers. You do not want them to think that by being vague you are trying to be evasive.
3. Most professions use special terms or jargon. For example, "ghosting" is used in one juvenile correctional facility together with the name of a midnight-shift employee (for example, "Terry's ghosting") to indicate that Terry cannot be

found and is probably sleeping somewhere. You may have picked up some of these terms during your internship. Before the interview, you may want to visit the library, access the Internet, or contact someone who is working in the field to become familiar with some of these professional terms.

Educational Background

Be prepared for the interviewer to ask the following questions about your educational background:

1. Why did you attend your particular college or university?
2. Of your courses, which did you enjoy and which did you least prefer, and why?
3. What were the most exciting times of your college career, and why?
4. What was your grade-point average? Was it as high as it could have been; if not, why not?
5. What kind of extracurricular activities and community service were you involved in?
6. Did you graduate on time? If not, why not?

Practice answering these questions before the interview and remember to communicate all answers as positively as possible.

Employment Experience

It will be obvious from your résumé whether you have an employment history. If you do, you may encounter such questions as these: What attracted you to your previous jobs, and what were your reasons for leaving? What kind of experience did you gain? What did you enjoy about the work, and what did you dislike? What kind of relationship did you have with your supervisor? What are you looking for in a job? Why are you attracted to this job? In answering these questions, you want to impress on the interviewer that you are ambitious, intelligent, and confident—in short, the best person for the job.

Long-Term Goals

When this questions arises, be prepared to answer it in generalities. At this time in your life, the interviewer will not expect you to have mapped out a 10- or 20-year plan. For example, you could respond that you are interested in pursuing a wide range of experiences that would assist in your professional development and that would eventually enable you to move into a leadership role in the organization. If these wide-ranging experiences include continuing your education and acquiring a graduate degree, discuss these aspirations in light of their empowering you to make worthwhile contributions to the organization and professional field.

CONTINUING EDUCATION

After graduation, some students choose to acquire a few years of criminal justice–related experience (especially those who have been hired by their internship agencies), while others enroll in law school or graduate programs in various disciplines. You will find that considering your career goals at the beginning of your internship experience comes in handy at this point because knowing your goals is crucial in determining the best graduate program for you. Students who are majoring in criminal justice–criminology may be interested in acquiring graduate degrees in criminal justice, criminology, social work, sociology, psychology, business or public administration, or the law. Once you have decided on the discipline, the next step is to learn which schools and programs fit your needs. If this information is not provided by your department, you may find graduate and law school directories that contain such pertinent information as descriptions of programs, academic requirements, costs, and locations in the university's library or career center.

The career center can also provide you with relevant information on deadlines for applications and required examinations. It is recommended that you make these inquiries at least a semester before you graduate. If you are considering law school, the earlier you inquire about the study programs available to assist you with the Law School Aptitude Test (LSAT), the better, since some students have had to repeat this examination to attain acceptable scores. Again, remember to get advice from your internship coordinator, other faculty members, and prelaw counselor in choosing a suitable discipline and school.

SUMMARY

In this chapter we have discussed issues related to determining the type of position you want, preparing a résumé that will help you obtain a position, locating the position, and preparing for interviews, as well as considerations related to graduate education.

To set your career goals, you have to assess your personal requirements, skills, and the geographic area in which you want to work. This chapter has covered several steps that will help you in evaluating these important areas. You will also find that the *Encyclopedia of Careers and Vocational Guidance* and the *Occupational Outlook Handbook* are two important sources of information on criminal justice and criminology-related occupations. Several factors to consider when updating or preparing a résumé are also discussed here, as are sources of information on job searches, including the Internet, which is the most current resource for locating employment information. Once you have completed the job search and have been offered an interview, follow closely the suggestions prepared here regarding your appearance, demeanor, communication skills, and other important factors discussed here.

Regardless of which path you choose, as you proceed down life's highway, periodically assess your personal aspirations, skills, and geographic choices, which may change over time as you expand your horizons and develop new professional and business relationships.

Concluding Comments

Throughout this book I have discussed your aspirations. In writing this book I have had three aspirations of my own that I want to share with you. First, I wanted to improve the caliber of internship training. Second, I wanted to organize and present the information in a way that it is easy to read and understand and that you can use during your internship and the transition to the professional world of work. Third, I wanted to include a resource guide of agencies in 25 major cities in the United States (the number of cities will increase in the next edition). This guide is provided at the back of this book. I welcome your comments, which will be helpful in writing the next edition, and I wish you success in your future careers.

Dorothy L. Taylor, Ph.D.
Department of Sociology
University of Miami
Miami, FL 33124-2208

References

Applebaum, P. S. "Statutes Regarding Patient–Therapist Sex." *Hospital and Community Psychiatry*, 41, 15–16. 1990.

Bairn, B., ed. *The Internship, Practicum, and Field Placement Handbook: A Guide for the Helping Professions*. Upper Saddle River, NJ: Prentice Hall, 1996.

Baker, R., and Meyer, F. A., Jr. *The Criminal Justice Game: Politics and Players*. North Scituate, MA: Duxbury Press, 1980.

Bankston, K. "Internship with the Bureau of Prisons." Unpublished manuscript, 1997.

Barnett, B. G. "The Mentor–Intern Relationship: Making the Most of Learning from Experience." *NASSP Bulletin*, 75 (May 1990):17–24.

Bennett, B. E., Bryant, B. K., VandenBos, G. R., and Greenwood, A. *Professional Liability and Risk Management*. Washington, DC: American Psychological Association, 1990.

Bent, A. E., *The Politics of Law Enforcement: Conflict and Power in Urban Communities*. Lexington, MA.: D.C. Heath, 1974.

Black, D. "The Legal Ins and Outs of Internship." *Perspective: The Campus Legal Monthly* (December 12, 1987):15–25.

Blackwelder, H. B., and Moorman, W. E. *Internships in Criminal Justice*. Raleigh, NC: Department of Administration, 1975–1976.

Blau, P. M. *Exchange and Power in Social Life*. New York: Wiley, 1964.

Boryrs, D. S., and Pope, K. S. "Dual Relationships between Therapist and Client: A National Study of Psychologists, Psychiatrists and Social Workers." *Professional Psychology: Research and Practice*, 20 (1989):232–242.

Carlson, N. A. *The Development of the Federal Prison System*. Washington, DC: Unicor, Federal Prison System, 1994.

Cecil, C. "Summer Internship: Florida Department of Corrections and Probation." Unpublished manuscript, 1996.

Chambliss, W. J. "Policing the Ghetto Underclass: The Politics of Law and Law Enforcement." *Social Problems*, 41 (1994):177–194.

Chastain, J. "The Summer Internship—What's in It for You." *The Black Collegian*, 92 (January–February 1990):179–180.

Clairborn, C. D., Berberoglu, L. S., Nerison, R. M., and Somberg, D. R. "The Client's Perspective: Ethical Judgments and Perceptions of Therapist's Practice." *Professional Psychology: Research and Practice*, 25 (1994):268–274.

Cole, G. F. "The Decision to Prosecute." *Law and Society Review*, 4, 331–344, 1970.

Cox, S. M., and Wade, J. E. *The Criminal Justice Network*, 3rd ed. New York: McGraw-Hill, 1998.

Dudley, J. S. "Learning through Field Experience." In O. Milton and Associates, eds., *On College Teaching*. San Francisco: Jossey-Bass, 1980, pp. 12–16.

Florida Department of Corrections. *Annual Report, 1995–1996*. Tallahassee, FL: Bureau of Research and Data Analysis, 1996.

Flowers, R. B., *Minorities and Criminality*. New York: Praeger, 1988.

Gifis, S. "Decision-making in a Prison Community." In B. Atkins and M. Pogrebin, eds., *The Invisible Justice System: Discretion and the Law*. Cincinnati, OH: Anderson Publishing, 1978.

Gordon, G. R., and McBride, B. *Criminal Justice Internships: Theory into Practice*, 2nd ed. Cincinnati, OH: Anderson, Publishing, 1990.

Greenberg, D. "Intern Hell." *The New Republic* (December 10, 1990):15–16.

Gutheil, T. G., and G. O. Gabbard. "The Concept of Boundaries in Clinical Practice: Theoretical and Risk Management Dimensions." *American Journal of Psychiatry*, 150, 1993, pp. 188–196.

Gutierrez, M. "My Internship Experience." Unpublished manuscript, 1997.

Hall, R. H. *Organizational Structure and Process*, 2nd ed. Upper Saddle River, NJ: Prentice Hall, 1977.

Henderson, M. B. "Family Intervention Specialty Program Internship." Unpublished manuscript, 1995.

Hersh, J. B. and K. Poey. "A Proposed Interviewing Guide for Intern Applicants." In R. H. Dana and W. T. May, eds., *Internship Training in Professional Psychology*. Washington, DC: Hemisphere Publishing Corporation, 1987, pp. 217–220.

Homa, M. "My Internship at the Bureau of Prisons." Unpublished manuscript, 1997.

Homestead Police Department. *Annual Report*. Homestead, FL: Homestead City Council, 1995.

Howing, P. T., and Wodarski, J. S. "Legal Requisites for Social Workers in Child Abuse and Neglect Situations." *Social Work*, 37 (1992):330–335.

Hoy, W. K. and Miskel, C. G. *Educational Administration: Theory, Research, and Practice*. New York: Random House, 1978.

Huling, R. Camp Manager, FCI Miami, Miami, FL. 1997.

"Industrial Internships Provide Physics Students with Valuable Experience." *Physics Today* (September 1991):93–94.

Jean, C. "Spring with ARISE." Unpublished manuscript, 1997.

Jorgenson, L., R. Randel, and L. Strasburger. "The Furor Over Psychotherapist–Patient Sexual Conduct: New Solutions to an Old Problem." *William and Mary Law Review*, 32, 643–729.

Kagle, J. D., and Giebelhausen, P. N. "Dual Relationships and Professional Boundaries." *Social Work*, 39(1994):213–220.

Keyman, F. I. *A Guide for Participation in University Internships in Law Enforcement*. Carbondale, IL: Southern Illinois University Press, December 1997.

Khoury, J. "An Overview of Internships." Unpublished manuscript, 1993.

Kitchener, K. S. "Intuition, Critical Evaluation and Ethical Principles: The Foundation for Ethical Decisions in Psychology." *The Counselor Psychologist*, 12 (1984):43–56.

Kitchener, K. S. "Dual Relationships: What Makes Them So Problematic?" *Journal of Counseling and Development*, 67 (1988):217–221.

Kleinig, J., and Smith, M. L. *Teaching Criminal Justice Ethics: Strategic Issues*. Cincinnati, OH: Anderson Publishing, 1997.

Kramer, M. "What Can Be Done?" *Time* (May 1, 1992):41–42.

LaFave, W., and Scott, A. W., Jr. *Criminal Law*. St. Paul, MN: West Publishing, 1972.

Lasswell, H. *Politics: Who Gets What, When, and How?* New York: Meridian, 1958.

Livingston, J. *Crime and Criminology*, 2nd ed. Upper Saddle River, NJ: Prentice Hall, 1996.

Livingston, E. "Secret Service Internship." Unpublished manuscript, 1997.

Lofland, J., and Lofland, L. *Analyzing Social Settings: A Guide to Qualitative Observation and Analysis*, 2nd ed. Belmont, CA: Wadsworth, 1984.

Mann, C. R. *Unequal Justice: A Question of Color*. Bloomington, IN: Indiana University Press, 1993.

Neubauer, D. W. *American's Courts and the Criminal Justice System*, 4th ed. Pacific Grove, CA: Brooks/Cole, 1992.

Newman, D. "Pleading Guilty for Considerations: A Study of Bargain Justice." *Journal of Criminal Law*, 37 (1970):665.

Nigro, F. A., and Nigro, L. G. *Modern Public Administration*. New York: Harper & Row, 1977.

Norcross, J. C., Strausser, D. J., and Faltus, F. J. "The Therapist's Therapist." *American Journal of Psychotherapy*, 42 (1988):53–66.

Nowell, D., and Spruill, J. "If It's Not Absolutely Confidential, Will Information Be Disclosed?" *Professional Psychology: Research and Practice*, 24 (1993):367–369.

Paradise, L. V., and Kirby, P. C. "Some Perspectives on the Legal Liability of Group Counseling in Private Practice." *Journal of Specialists in Group Work*, 2 (1990):114–118.

Permaul, J. "Monitoring and Supporting Experimental Learning." Washington, DC: National Society for Internships and Experimental Education, 1981.

Perrow, C. "The Analysis of Goals in Complex Organizations." *American Sociological Review*, 26 (April 1961): 854–865.

Pitts, J. H. "Organizing a Practicum and Internship Program in Counselor Education." *Counselor Education and Supervision*, 31 (1992):196–207.

Pope, K. S., and Vetter, V. V. "Ethical Dilemmas Encountered by Members of the American Psychological Association: A National Survey." *American Psychologist*, 47 (1992):397–411.

Rubanowitz, D. E. "Public Attitudes Toward Psychotherapist–Client Confidentiality." *Professional Psychology: Research and Practice*, 18, 613–618, 1987.

Santos, G. "Internship Report—Guardian Ad Litem." Unpublished manuscript, 1997.

Schultz, M. "Internships in Sociology: Liability Issues and Risk Management Measures." *Teaching Sociology*, 20 (July 1992): 183–191.

Scott, F. G. "Action Theory and Research in Social Organization." *American Journal of Sociology*, 64 (January 1959):386–395.

Scott, M. E. "Internships Add Value to College Recruitment." *Personnel Journal* (April 1992):59–63.

Stadler, H. and R. D. Paul. "Counselor Educators' Preparation In Ethics." *Journal of Counseling and Development*, 64, 328–330, 1986.

Strasburger, L. H., Jorgenson, L., and Randles, R. "Criminalization of Psychotherapist–Patient Sex." *American Journal of Psychiatry*, 148 (1991):859–863.

Suelzle, M., and Borzak, L. "Stages of Fieldwork." In L. Borzak, ed., *Field Study: A Sourcebook for Experimental Learning*. Thousand Oaks, CA: Sage Publications, 1981.

Swenson, L. C. *Psychology and Law for the Helping Professions*. Pacific Grove, CA: Brooks/Cole, 1993.

Taylor, D. L., and R. L. Bing III. "Racial Discrimination in the Juvenile Justice System: Some Unanswered Questions" *Challenge* (Dec) 6 (2):5–28, 1995.

Taylor, D. L., F. Biafora, Jr., and G. Warheit. "Racial Mistrust and Disposition to Deviance Among African American, Haitian, and other Caribbean Island Adolescent Boys." *Law and Human Behavior*, 18 (3):291–303, 1994.

U.S. Department of Justice. *A Judicial Guide to the Bureau of Prisons*. Ray Brook, NY: Federal Bureau of Prisons, 1991.

U.S. Department of Justice. *Bureau of Prisons Goals for 1995 and Beyond*. Lompoc, CA: Federal Bureau of Prisons, 1995.

Vesper, J. H., and Brock, G. W. *Ethics, Legalities, and Professional Practice Issues in Marriage and Family Therapy.* Needham Heights, MA: Allyn and Bacon, 1990.

Walsh, J. A. "From Clinician to Supervisor: Essential Ingredients for Training." *Families in Society,* 71 (2) (1990):82–87.

Walters, L. S. "Anticrime Wave Shackles State Educational Spending." *The Christian Science Monitor* (February 1995):2–11.

Weber, M. *The Theory of Social and Economic Organization.* London: William Hodge, 1947.

Wennes, L. B. "Find Work Now to Dazzle Employers Later." *National Business Employment Weekly* (Spring/Summer 1993):31–32.

Wilson, J. Q., *Varieties of Police Behavior.* Cambridge: Harvard University Press, 1968.

Woodward, B., and Armstrong, S. *The Brethren: Inside the Supreme Court.* New York: Simon and Schuster, 1979.

Zakutansky, T. J. and E. A. Sirles. "Ethical and Legal Issues in Field Education: Shared Responsibility and Risk. *Journal of Social Work Education,* 29, 338–347, 1993.

Index

Resource Guide

In this guide we list various criminal justice agencies that will assist you in entering the world of work in 25 major cities in the United States taken from the *Statistical Abstract of the United States 1996: The National Data Book*. The agencies represented here are Federal Bureau of Investigation (FBI), juvenile justice agencies, police departments, probation and parole offices, and the Secret Service. This listing represents only a small number of criminal justice agencies but does provide a valuable starting point.

1. New York, NY

    FBI
    26 Federal Plaza, 23rd Floor
    New York, NY 10278
    (212) 384-1000

    Department of Juvenile Justice
    365 Broadway
    New York, NY 10007
    (212) 925-7779

    Department of Probation
    115 Leonard Street
    New York, NY 10013
    (212) 442-4293

    Department of Parole
    3114 West 40th Street
    New York, NY 10018
    (212) 239-6000

    Police Department
    41 Main Street
    New York, NY 10044-0052
    (518) 762-3143

    U.S. Secret Service
    6 World Trade Center
    New York, NY 10048-0206
    (212) 637-4500

2. Los Angeles, CA

    FBI
    11000 Wilshire Boulevard
    Los Angeles, CA 90024-3602
    (310) 477-6565

    Juvenile Detention
    1605 East Lake Avenue
    Los Angeles, CA 90033-1009
    (213) 226-8616

    Probation Office
    312 North Spring Street
    Los Angeles, CA 90012

    Department of Parole
    107 South Broadway
    Los Angeles, CA 90012-4402

    Police Department
    110 East Ninth Street
    Los Angeles, CA 90079
    (213) 624-6042

U.S. Secret Service
255 East Temple Street
Los Angeles, CA 90012
(213) 894-4830

3.   Chicago, IL

FBI
219 South Dearborn Street,
    Suite 905
Chicago, IL 60604-1705
(312) 431-1333

Juvenile Tempy Detention Center
1100 South Hampton Avenue
Chicago, IL 60612-4207
(312) 738-8200

Department of Probation
2600 South California Avenue
Chicago, IL 60608
(773) 869-3280

Department of Parole
2600 South California Avenue
Chicago, IL 60608
(773) 869-3300

Police Department
2259 South Damen Avenue
Chicago, IL 60606-6613
(312) 353-2212

U.S. Secret Service
300 South Riverside Plaza
Chicago, IL 60606-6613
(312) 353-5431

4.   Houston, TX

FBI
2500 ETC Jester Boulevard,
    Suite 200
Houston, TX 77008-1300
(713) 868-2266

Juvenile Division
201 Fannin Street
Houston, TX 77002-1901
(713) 755-5874

Department of Probation
515 Rusk Street
Houston, TX 77002
(713) 250-5266

Department of Parole
515 Rusk Street
Houston, TX 77002
(713) 250-5300

Police Department
61 Riesner Road
Houston, TX 77058-3502
(713) 222-3131

U.S. Secret Service
602 Sawyer Street
Houston, TX 77007-7510
(713) 868-2299

5.   Pittsburgh, PA

FBI
700 Grant Street, Suite 300
Pittsburgh, PA 15219-1906
(412) 471-2000

Juvenile Detention Home
7150 Highland Drive
Pittsburgh, PA 15206-1206
(412) 661-6806

Department of Probation
1520 Penn Avenue
Pittsburgh, PA 15222-4325
(412) 350-2320

Board of Parole
100–102 Ten Circle West
Pittsburgh, PA 15233
(412) 645-7000

Police Department
3731 Burrows Street
Pittsburgh, PA 15213
(412) 687-8656

U.S. Secret Service
1000 Liberty Avenue
Pittsburgh, PA 15290
(412) 644-3384

6.   San Diego, CA

FBI
915 Second Avenue, Suite 710
San Diego, CA 92101-8897
(619) 231-1122

Juvenile Justice Department
324 Apple Still Road
San Diego, CA 92101
(619) 531-2495

Department of Probation
4004 Kearny Mesa Road
San Diego, CA 92110-3730
(619) 560-1837

Department of Parole
4004 Kearny Mesa Road
San Diego, CA 92110-3730
(619) 560-1850

Police Department
1401 Broadway
San Diego, CA 92101
(619) 521-2777

U.S. Secret Service
550 West C Street, Suite 660
San Diego, CA 92101
(619) 557-5640

7. Phoenix, AZ

FBI
201 East Indianaola Avenue,
   Suite 400
Phoenix, AZ 85012
(602) 279-5511

Department of Juvenile Justice
1624 West Adams Street
Phoenix, AZ 85007
(602) 542-3987

Department of Probation
1022 East Garfield Street
Phoenix, AZ 85006-3236
(602) 254-7030

Office of Parole
6725 35th Street
Phoenix, AZ 85017
(602) 255-4147

Police Department
12220 North 39th Avenue
Phoenix, AZ 85029-3100
(602) 495-5009

U.S. Secret Service
3200 North Central Avenue,
   Suite 2180
Phoenix, AZ 85012
(602) 640-5580

8. Dallas, TX

FBI
1801 North Lamar Street,
   Suite 300
Dallas, TX 75202-1795
(214) 720-2200

Juvenile Hall
2600 Lone Star Drive
Dallas, TX 75212
(214) 698-2200

Division of Probation
3650 North Buckner Boulevard
Dallas, TX 75228
(214) 320-9713

Division of Parole
3650 North Buckner Boulevard
Dallas, TX 75228
(214) 320-9715

Police Department
2014 Main Street
Dallas, TX 75201
(214) 670-3011

U.S. Secret Service
125 East John W. Carpenter
   Freeway
Dallas, TX 75201
(214) 670-3011

9. San Antonio, TX

FBI
615 East Houston Street,
   Suite 200
San Antonio, TX 78205-2040
(210) 225-6741

Juvenile Detention Center
600 Mission Road
San Antonio, TX 78210
(210) 531-1100

Department of Probation
655 East Durango Boulevard
San Antonio, TX 78206-1102
(210) 554-7200

Office of Parole
655 East Durango Boulevard
San Antonio, TX 78206-1102
(210) 554-7300

Police Department
214 West Neuva
San Antonio, TX 78207-4514
(210) 207-7615

U.S. Secret Service
727 East Durango Boulevard
San Antonio, TX 78206-1204
(210) 472-6175

10.   Detroit, MI

FBI
477 Michigan Avenue,
   26th Floor
Detroit, MI 48226
(313) 965-2323

Juvenile Detention Center
1333 East Forest
Detroit, MI 48207
(313) 833-2905

Department of Probation
426 Clinton Street
Detroit, MI 48226
(313) 224-5000

Office of Parole
1200 Sixth Street
Detroit, MI 48226
(313) 256-2566

Police Department
1300 Beaubien Street
Detroit, MI 48226
(313) 596-2200

U.S. Secret Service
477 Michigan Avenue, 10th
Floor
Detroit, MI 48226-2719
(313) 226-6400

11.   San Jose, CA

FBI
280 South First Street
San Jose, CA 95113-3002
(408) 998-5633

Juvenile Hall
840 Guadalupe Parkway
San Jose, CA 95110-1714
(408) 299-3481

Office of Probation
280 South First Street
San Jose, CA 95113-3002
(408) 291-7671

Office of Parole
165 Lewis Road
San Jose, CA 95111-2158
(408) 629-5980

Police Department
55 West Younger Avenue
San Jose, CA 95110
(408) 211-2220

U.S. Secret Service
280 South First Street,
   Suite 2050
San Jose, CA 95113
(408) 535-5288

12.   Indianapolis, IN

FBI
575 North Pennsylvania Street,
   Suite 679
Indianapolis, IN 46204-1524
(317) 639-3301

Juvenile Corrections Facility
2596 Girl's School Road
Indianapolis, IN 46214-2105
(317) 244-3887

Office of Probation
200 East Washington Street,
   Suite 641
Indianapolis, IN 46204
(317) 327-4252

Indianapolis Parole Office
3921 North Meridian Street
Indianapolis, IN 46208-4011
(317) 931-4375

Police Department
209 East Street Joseph Street
Indianapolis, IN 46204
(317) 327-6500

U.S. Secret Service
575 North Pennsylvania Street,
    Suite 211
Indianapolis, IN 46204-1524
(317) 226-6444

13.   San Francisco, CA

FBI
450 Golden Gate Avenue,
    13th Floor
San Francisco, CA 94105
(415) 744-9026

Juvenile Office of San Mateo
21 Tower Road
San Francisco, CA 94127
(650) 312-8816

Department of Probation
850 Bryant Street
San Francisco, CA 94103-4603
(415) 553-1704

Department of Parole
850 Bryant Street
San Francisco, CA 94103-4603
(415) 553-1689

Police Department
766 Vallejo Street
San Francisco, CA 94133-3818
(415) 553-1532

U.S. Secret Service
345 Spear Street, Suite 530
San Francisco, CA 94105
(415) 744-9020

14.   Baltimore, MD

FBI
7142 Ambassador Road
Baltimore, MD 21244-2754
(410) 265-8080

Department of Juvenile Services
3939 Reisterstown Road
Baltimore, MD 21215-7601
(410) 333-6041

Probation Field Office
217 East Fayette Street
Baltimore, MD 21202-3410
(410) 798-4834

Parole Field Office
217 East Fayette Street
Baltimore, MD 21202-3410
(410) 798-3400

Police Department
601 East Fayette Street
Baltimore, MD 21202
(410) 396-2525

U.S. Secret Service
100 South Charles Street
Baltimore, MD 21201-2725
(410) 962-2200

15.   Jacksonville, FL

FBI
7820 Arlington Expressway
Jacksonville, FL 32211-7481
(904) 721-1211

Juvenile Detention Center
1241 East Eighth Street
Jacksonville, FL 32206
(904) 798-4834

Department of Probation
4250 Lake Side Drive
Jacksonville, FL 32210
(904) 381-6000

Department of Parole
4250 Lake Side Drive
Jacksonville, FL 32210
(904) 381-6100

Police Department
501 East Bay Street
Jacksonville, FL 32203
(904) 630-7600

U.S. Secret Service
7820 Arlington Expressway
Jacksonville, FL 32211-7481
(904) 724-4530

16.   Columbus, OH

FBI
500 South Front Street, Suite 1050
Columbus, OH 43215
(614) 224-1183

Juvenile Detention Facility
399 South Front Street
Columbus, OH 43215-4591
(614) 462-4490

Department of Probation Services
373 South High Street
Columbus, OH 43215-4591
(614) 462-3700

Office of Parole
1050 Freeway Drive North
Columbus, OH 43229
(614) 752-1253

Police Department
1611 Chillicothe Street
Columbus, OH 43207
(614) 491-3211

U.S. Secret Service
300 Hancock Street
Columbus, OH 43215
(419) 625-6052

17.   Milwaukee, WI

FBI
330 East Kilbourn Avenue,
   Suite 600
Milwaukee, WI 53202-3144
(414) 276-4684

Juvenile Services
3936 North Murray Avenue
Milwaukee, WI 53211-2303
(414) 332-0924

Division of Probation
1673 South Ninth Street
Milwaukee, WI 53204
(414) 382-7800

Division of Parole
1673 South Ninth Street
Milwaukee, WI 53204
(414) 382-8000

Police Department
3400 North Maryland Avenue
Milwaukee, WI 53211-2903
(414) 229-4123

U.S. Secret Service
517 West Wisconsin Avenue
Milwaukee, WI 53211
(414)-297-3587

18.   Memphis, TN

FBI
225 North Humphreys
   Boulevard, Suite 300
Memphis, TN 38120-2107
(901) 747-4300

Juvenile Justice Center
616 Adams Avenue
Memphis, TN 38105
(901) 528-8400

Probation Services, Inc.
2959 Elmore Park Road
Memphis, TN 38134-8309
(901) 37705529

Office of Parole
1358 Madison Avenue
Memphis, TN 38104
(901) 543-6566

Police Department
201 Poplar Avenue
Memphis, TN 38103
(901) 528-2222

U.S. Secret Service
5350 Poplar Avenue
Memphis, TN 38119
(901) 544-0333

19.   El Paso, TX

FBI
700 East San Antonio, Suite 600
El Paso, TX 79901-7020
(915) 533-7451

Juvenile Justice Center
6400 Delta Drive
El Paso, TX 79905-5408
(915) 775-4773

Department of Probation
7145 Industrial Avenue
El Paso, TX 79915-1224
(915) 778-4233

Office of Parole
5929 Brook Hollow Drive
El Paso, TX 79925-1810
(915) 778-4250

Police Department
14999 Darrington Road
El Paso, TX 79927-7348
(915) 852-1047

U.S. Secret Service
4849 North Mesa Street
El Paso, TX 79912-5936
(915) 533-6950

20.   Washington, DC

FBI
1900 Half Street SW
Washington, DC 20024
(202) 252-7801

Youth Center Corrections
   Department
1923 Vermont Avenue, NW
Washington, DC 20001-4103
(202) 643-2234

Office of Probation
401 New York Avenue NE
Washington, DC 20001-4628
(202) 675-9183

Office of Parole
717 14th Street NW
Washington, DC 20005-3203
(202) 727-2264

Police Department
320 First Street NW
Washington, DC 20001
(202) 727-9334

U.S. Secret Service
1050 Connecticut Ave NW
Washington, DC 20036-5303
(202) 435-5100

21.   Boston, MA

FBI
One Center Plaza, Suite 600
Boston, MA 02108
(617) 742-5533

Juvenile Center
450 Canterbury Street
Boston, MA 02131-3216
(617) 727-2264

Office of Probation
507 New Court House
Temperton Square
Boston, MA 02108
(617) 725-8426

Office of Parole
27043 Wormwood Street
Boston, MA 02210
(617) 727-3272

Police Department
City Hall
Boston, MA 02201
(906) 482-3100

U.S. Secret Service
10 Causeway Street
Boston, MA 02108
(617) 565-5640

22.   Seattle, WA

FBI
280 South Second Avenue,
   Suite 710
Seattle, WA 98174-1096
(206) 622-0460

Juvenile Center
210 Dexter Avenue North
Seattle, WA 98109
(206) 328-5693

Office of Probation
1010 Fifth Avenue
Seattle, WA 98104-1130
(206) 442-7435

Office of Parole
1010 Fifth Avenue
Seattle, WA 98104-1130
(206) 442-7400

Police Department
601 Third Avenue
Seattle, WA 98104
(206) 684-8917

U.S. Secret Service
915 Second Avenue, Room 890
Seattle, WA 98174
(206) 220-6800

23.   Nashville, TN

FBI
3322 West End Avenue
Nashville, TN 37203
(615) 292-4489

Juvenile Detention Center
100 Woodland Street
Nashville, TN 37213-1215
(615) 862-8066

Department of Probation
100 James Robertson Parkway,
    Room 21
Nashville, TN 37201
(615) 862-8380

Office of Parole
404 James Robertson Parkway
Nashville, TN 37201
(615) 741-1673

Police Department
200 James Robertson Parkway
Nashville, TN 37201
(615) 862-8600

U.S. Secret Service
658 U.S. Court House
801 Broadway
Nashville, TN 37203
(615) 736-5841

24.   Denver, CO

FBI
1961 Stout Street, Suite 1823
Denver, CO 80294
(303) 629-7171

Juvenile Corrections
4255 South Knox Court
Denver, CO 80236
(303) 866-7345

Department of Probation
303 West Colfax Avenue
Denver, CO 80204
(303) 640-2971

Office of Parole
116 Inverness Drive East
Englewood, CO 80112
(303) 784-6126

Police Department
4685 Peoria Street
Denver, CO 80239
(303) 576-2897

U.S. Secret Service
1660 Lincoln Street
Denver, CO 80264-3101
(303) 866-1010

25. Austin, TX

FBI
9420 Research Boulevard
Echelon III, Suite 400
Austin, TX 78759
(512) 345-1111

Juvenile Center
2515 South Congress Avenue
Austin, TX 78704-5513
(512) 448-7000

Department of Probation
411 West 13th Street
Austin, TX 78701
(512) 708-4600

Department of Pardons and
    Parole
8610 Shoal Creek Boulevard
Austin, TX 78758
(512) 406-5200

Police Department
715 East Eighth Street
Austin, TX 78701
(512) 480-5000

U.S. Secret Service
300 East Eighth Street
Austin, TX 78701-3204
(512) 482-5103